Phonemic Awareness
Activities & Games
for Early Learners

c/a/t

kitten

mitten

Author

Beth Anne Bray, M.S.Ed

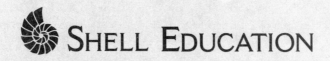

SHELL EDUCATION

Credits

Editor
Angela Cybulski, M.A.

Project Manager
Jodene Smith, M.A.

Assistant Editor
Leslie Huber, M.A.

Editorial Director
Dona Herweck Rice

Editor-in-Chief
Sharon Coan, M.S.Ed.

Editorial Manager
Gisela Lee, M.A.

Creative Director
Lee Aucoin

Cover Design
Lee Aucoin

Cover Artist
Amy Couch

Illustration Manager/ Designer
Timothy J. Bradley

Artists
Timothy J. Bradley
Ana Clark
Mira Fraser
Chris Sabatino

Print Production
Sandra Riley

Publisher
Corinne Burton, M.A.Ed.

Standards Compendium, Copyright 2004 McREL. www.mcrel.org/standards-benchmarks

Shell Education
5301 Oceanus Drive
Huntington Beach, California 92649
http://www.shelleducation.com

ISBN 978-1-4258-0144-1

© 2007 Shell Education

Table of Contents

Introduction and Rationale

Educators and parents alike want to know how best to help children succeed in learning to read. After years of research, we know that reading is a multifaceted skill. Phonemic awareness is one important skill to help children develop a strong foundation for becoming successful readers. Young children benefit from fun, playful listening and speaking activities that help them acquire strong pre-reading skills. *Phonemic Awareness Activities & Games for Early Learners* is an excellent resource for assisting classroom teachers and parents in providing emergent readers with developmentally appropriate games and activities for pre-reading skill building.

Phonemic awareness allows children to make the leap between listening and speaking to reading and writing. Most adults take for granted this huge mental shift, which is the difference between phonemic awareness and phonics. Phonemic awareness, a skill children learn very early in life, is essentially an awareness of the smallest units of sounds, or phonemes. Phonemic awareness in children refers to their ability to hear and identify different sounds in oral language. Phonics, on the other hand, is the understanding that there is a relationship between the sounds in spoken language and the letters and spelling patterns that represent these sounds in written language. Phonemes are the building blocks of language. Combined, phonemes make syllables, which then combine to make discrete words, which are finally combined to create sentence structures capable of expressing and extending thoughts and meaning. Children learn to speak without necessarily learning these basic units of words or phonemes. In speaking, words and phrases are the units of meaning. For example, children learn milk is something used for drinking (Adams, 1990; Yopp, 1992), but they do not learn milk is also a word, made up of distinct and abstract sounds, /m/ /i/ /l/ /k/ that need to come together in just the right way to create meaning.

Children need to learn the relationship between speaking and reading and writing. A strong foundation in the patterns of oral language helps children as they learn the abstract sound/symbol correspondence necessary to read and write successfully. When children are given explicit instruction to develop phonemic awareness, they are better able to recognize patterns and sound/symbol relationships, and manipulate sounds to speak and read novel words. There is a significant body of research presented over the last 20 years that supports explicit instruction in phonemic awareness as a key component in reading and writing success. Phonemic awareness plays a critical role in learning skills for word recognition and spelling (Griffith & Olson, 1992) and researchers say phonemic awareness is a strong predictor of later reading achievement (Juel, 1988; Juel, Griffith, & Gough, 1986; Lomax & McGee, 1987; Tunmer & Nesdale, 1985).

Instruction in phonemic awareness is an auditory and verbal exercise that can be broken down into tasks that build on one another. At the simplest level, children learn to determine if pairs of words rhyme. Next, children will be able to match, isolate, and blend sounds. At the highest level, children will manipulate the sounds in words to create new words by adding, deleting, and substituting sounds (i.e., *clamp* without the /c/ sound is the word *lamp*). Based on careful analysis of the phonemic awareness tasks recommended by leading researchers (Yopp, 1992; Griffith & Olson, 1992; CIERA, 2001), the activities in this book have been organized from the simplest level to the most demanding. The first building block is Rhyming, the ability to recognize words that rhyme and do not rhyme, as well as creating rhyming words using onset and rimes. The next level is Syllabication, referring to the ability to break up words into syllables and to count syllables. This leads to Sound Matching where children recognize words that begin with the same sound, identify a word with a specific sound in a list of words, and identify a word that sounds different from other words in a list. These levels prepare children to develop the skill of Sound Isolation that is so important for reading and spelling. Sound isolation involves identifying a word that begins with a specific sound from a word list and recognizing the beginning, middle, and ending sounds of words. Proficiency in Sound Isolation leads to Sound Blending, the ability to combine individual sounds to make words. Higher levels of phonemic awareness include Sound Segmentation—the ability to identify the individual sounds in words—and Sound Manipulation, which allows children to create new words by deleting, adding, or substituting sounds in words.

Phonemic awareness activities are best presented one task at a time, lasting for not more than 15- to 20-minute sessions. It is important to focus on one skill at a time while working through the lessons from rhyming to sound manipulation. Mastery of one skill level provides a strong foundation on which to introduce, build, and develop higher level skills. Bradley and Bryant (1983) concluded that phonemic awareness instruction is especially powerful when combined with instruction in the alphabetic principle. Activities in this book include adaptations for alphabet and phonics activities for those children who are developmentally ready for these lessons.

The activities and games in this book rely on oral response and listening exercises presented in a whimsical way. The activities use familiar rhymes and tunes along with games that the children can play in large and small groups. Griffith and Olson (1992) and Yopp (1992) advocate phonemic awareness activities, which are playful and game-like. Many experts encourage teachers and parents to provide children with language stimulation above and beyond listening and speaking in the preschool and early school years, which include word games, rhymes, and riddles (Mattingly, 1984). Children need to interact with each other and use their natural curiosity to "play" with language. This book includes a variety of ways for children to experiment with sounds and words and have fun at the same time.

Each activity in this book includes picture cards and/or word lists to make the preparation of a comprehensive phonemic awareness program simple for teachers or parents of young children.

The activities increase in sophistication and the suggested word lists build in complexity. The lists promote vocabulary development, offer a variety of onset and rimes, and include consonant-vowel-consonant (CVC) words, short and long vowel words, as well as words with blends and digraphs. Please note, the word lists and picture cards are not exhaustive by any means, but are suggested lists for ease in using the activities. Each activity has a list of adaptations to fit the needs of your classroom.

This book will easily fit with any language arts program you are currently using. You will have a wide variety of activities to choose from when teaching the crucial skills of phonemic awareness. Play, enjoy, and learn!

How to Use This Book

Selecting Activities and Games

The activities and games in this book are divided into six sections: **Rhyming and Syllabication, Sound Matching, Sound Isolation, Sound Blending, Sound Segmentation,** and **Sound Manipulation**. See the table of contents for specific page numbers on which each section begins. The games and activities are presented in the order of acquisition for children. Most students will benefit by practicing the skills in the order presented in this book. Begin by reviewing the activities and games according to the skill you desire; however, do not be limited by the sections. Many of the activities and games in this book can be adapted to address other skills. For example, the activity "Sorting Bags" is in the Sound Matching section of the book; however, the activity can easily be adapted to allow students to practice sound segmentation. Some suggestions for adaptations are provided for each game.

Preparation and Storage

The materials needed for each activity or game are listed on the teacher-direction pages. Specific patterns or game boards that may be needed are on the pages following the teacher directions. The patterns can be photocopied in black and white from this book and then colored by hand, or they can be printed in full color from the CD. Glue the pieces to construction paper or thin cardboard to create more durable pieces. Consider laminating all the pieces for durability, too. Enlarging the patterns and game boards is another option you may wish to consider. Use a copy machine with an enlarge option or copy the pattern onto a transparency. Place the transparency on an overhead projector and trace the image onto a piece of poster board.

A 9" x 12" (23 cm x 30 cm) manila envelope with a clasp works well to store most of the pieces needed for each game. You may want to create an envelope for each game in order to keep the pieces organized and easy to access. Be sure to clearly label each envelope with the name of the game. Once the materials needed to play the game are gathered and the game pieces created, preparation for the activities and games is minimal. Consider photocopying the teacher-direction page and cutting out the "Activity Procedure." Glue these to the front of the manila envelope. These directions tell how to do the activity or to play the game. The envelope can then be handed to a parent volunteer or classroom aide with minimal verbal directions because everything needed is contained within the envelope.

Introducing the Activities and Games

Even though many of the games are designed for a small group, you may wish to introduce the activities and games in a whole-class setting. You may have to select a few students to help you demonstrate how to do the activity or play the game, or you may be able to modify the activity slightly in order to accommodate the whole class. An overhead projector is another method of introducing an activity or game to the whole class. Photocopy necessary patterns onto transparencies, which can then be projected on a screen for the whole class to see. Finally, the activities and games can be introduced in a small group. Be sure to consistently describe and play the game with each group so that when the children play the game independently they will all play by the same rules. The specific needs of your class and the particular activity will help you decide which method of introduction is the best one for your students.

It is useful to remind students each time an activity or game is introduced or played that the purpose is to practice reading, not to see who can win. Everyone wins if letters, sounds, and sight words are learned and practiced in a fun way. You may wish to make it a policy that all students get a sticker, kudos from the teacher, or other small prizes if they participate in the activity or game. This reinforces the fact that everyone is a winner when he or she practices reading.

Parent Volunteers and Classroom Aides

Utilize parent volunteers and classroom aides to assist you in preparing the materials in this book. Often, parents who are unable to volunteer in the classroom are willing to assist in coloring or assembling materials that are sent home.

Be sure to provide specific directions and all of the materials necessary for the volunteers to complete the task correctly. Providing volunteers with a "return by [date]" slip also helps you get the materials back in a timely manner.

Parent volunteers, classroom aides, and cross-age tutors are excellent resources to monitor small groups as they play games. Provide any game monitors with directions on how the activity is to be done or how the games are to be played. Remind the monitors that the purpose of the activity or game is to practice reading.

Who Goes First?

Who goes first? This is probably one of the most hotly contested questions when children play games. You will want to have this question answered prior to introducing an activity or game to the students. You may wish to have a set procedure for all the activities and games that can be used for determining who goes first, or you may wish to select a different procedure for each activity and game. Either way, having the procedure established will eliminate many arguments. Some suggestions for determining who goes first are:

- Roll a die.
- Draw straws.
- Pull numbers out of a hat or other container.
- Flip a coin.
- Play rock, paper, scissors.
- Choose the person wearing the most items of clothing of a selected color.
- Have the youngest/oldest go first.
- Have ladies/gentlemen go first.

Correlation to Standards

The No Child Left Behind (NCLB) legislation mandates that all states adopt academic standards that identify the skills students will learn in kindergarten through grade 12. While many states had already adopted academic standards prior to NCLB, the legislation set requirements to ensure the standards were detailed and comprehensive.

Standards are designed to focus instruction and guide adoption of curricula. Standards are statements that describe the criteria necessary for students to meet specific academic goals. They define the knowledge, skills, and content students should acquire at each level. Standards are also used to develop standardized tests to evaluate students' academic progress.

In many states today, teachers are required to demonstrate how their lessons meet state standards. State standards are used in the development of Shell Education products, so educators can be assured that they meet the academic requirements of each state.

How to Find Your State Correlations

SEP is committed to producing educational materials that are research- and standards-based. In this effort, all products are correlated to the academic standards of the 50 states, the District of Columbia, and the Department of Defense Dependent Schools. A correlation report customized for your state can be printed directly from the following website: http://www.shelleducation.com. If you require assistance in printing correlation reports, please contact Customer Service at 1-800-877-3450.

McREL Compendium

SEP uses the Mid-continent Research for Education and Learning (McREL) Compendium to create standards correlations. Each year, McREL analyzes state standards and revises the compendium. By following this procedure, they are able to produce a general compilation of national standards.

Each phonemic awareness activity in this book is based on one or more content standard. The chart shows the standards that correlate to each lesson used in the book. To see a state-specific correlation, visit the Shell Education website at http://www.shelleducation.com.

Correlation to Standards Chart

Phonological Awareness

Standard: Uses listening and speaking strategies for different purposes	
Benchmark	**Lesson and Page Number**
Discriminates among the sounds of spoken language (McREL, Language Arts 8.15)	All activities 12–171
Knows rhyming sounds and simple rhymes (e.g., identifies rhymes and rhyming sounds) (McREL, Language Arts 8.16)	Pep Step Rhyme .... 12–17 Higglety Pigglety Pop .... 18–21 Go Rhyme ....22–29 Funny Bunny ....30–35 Who Belongs? 70-75
Knows that words are made up of sounds (e.g., that words can begin alike, sound alike) (McREL, Language Arts 8.17)	All activities 12–171
Identify and repeat individual sounds in words	Higglety Pigglety Pop .... 18–21 All activities in Sound Matching ....48–75 All activities in Sound Isolation .... 76–103 All activities in Sound Blending ....104–125 All activities in Sound Segmentation ....126–149 All activities in Sound Manipulation 150–171
Identify the same sound in different words or phrases	All activities in Sound Matching ....48–75 All activities in Sound Isolation .... 76–103 All activities in Sound Blending ....104–125 All activities in Sound Segmentation ....126–149 All activities in Sound Manipulation 150–171
Identify from a list the word/sound that does not belong	All activities in Sound Blending.................104–125

Phonological Awareness

Standard: Uses listening and speaking strategies for different purposes	
Benchmark	**Lesson and Page Number**
Combine sounds to make a word	All activities in Sound Blending...........................104–125
Say a word by individual sounds	All activities in Sound Segmentation..................126–149
Manipulate words by adding, deleting, or substituting sounds	Button Slide ....154–157 Tap, Tap, Run..158–159 Name Change..160–163 Big Bug ....164–167 Magic Word...168–171
Knows that words are made up of syllables (McREL, Language Arts 8.18)	Syllable Sort...36–43 Clap, Snap, Tap..44–47
Listens to a variety of fiction, nonfiction, poetry, drama, rhymes, and songs (McREL, Language Arts 8.19)	Pep Step Rhyme...12–17 Higglety Pigglety Pop ....18–21 Go Rhyme..22–29 Funny Bunny..30–35 Who Belongs? ....70–75 Little Boy Blue ....84–87 Listen and Act...96–103 The Turtle and the Hares.....................................104–107 Mary Had a Little Word ....118–121 I Can Say...146–149 Nursery Rhymes 173–176

Observing Students for Assessment

Take advantage of the great opportunity to assess students as you observe them participating in phonemic awareness activities or playing phonics games. There are a variety of assessment tools, such as checklists, anecdotal notes, and data-capture sheets, that can be used for documenting observations. Data-capture sheets are especially helpful to document events, behaviors, and skills. These sheets can then be used to provide an overall picture of what a student is capable of and areas in which the student still needs to develop. Data-capture sheets usually incorporate a checklist of specific behaviors to be observed and space for observation notes. Below is a general form that can be used as you observe students participating in phonemic awareness activities and games. The first two observations are general observations that can be applied to almost any activity or game. Fill in the bottom two observations to include specific skills to observe, such as "Confuses 'b' and 'd' sounds."

Y = Yes, behavior exhibited   S = behavior somewhat exhibited   N = behavior not exhibited

Student Name _____ Date_____

	Y	S	N	
1.	❑	❑	❑	Exhibited an adequate understanding of the activity/game.
2.	❑	❑	❑	Displayed knowledge of vocabulary related to the activity/game.
3.	❑	❑	❑	_____
4.	❑	❑	❑	_____

Overall, the student's performance [circle choice] expectations...

went beyond   met overall   met partial   met minimal   did not meet

Notes:

Pep Step Rhyme

Skill:

Rhyming

Suggested Group Size:

4–10 students

Activity Overview:

Students will recognize rhyming word pairs and step forward or backward.

Materials:

- "Rhyming Word Pair Cards" (pages 14–16)
- "Non-Rhyming Word Pair Cards" (page 17)
- chalk or string to designate finish line

Activity Preparation

1. Photocopy both "Rhyming Word Pair Cards" and "Non-Rhyming Word Pair Cards" onto cardstock paper (or print copies from the CD).

2. Cut out the cards.

3. Laminate the cards for durability, if desired.

4. Identify a space large enough for the students to safely move ten steps forward and backward.

5. Select a starting point and designate a finish line.

6. Once selected, mark both starting point and finish line with chalk or string.

Activity Procedure

1. Have the students line up side-by-side (shoulder-to-shoulder) in the area of the classroom or playground you have selected for this activity.

2. Say to the students, "If it is a rhyme you hear, take a giant step near. If the words do not rhyme, then you must step back this time."

3. Select and read a word pair from the stack of cards.

4. Continue repeating the instruction and reading the word pair cards, having the students step forward or back according to what they hear. Be sure to occasionally alternate rhyming word pairs with non-rhyming word pairs to allow students an opportunity to practice differentiating between word sounds.

5. When you want the game to end, select enough rhyming word pair cards in a row for the students to reach the finish line.

Adaptations

- Use as a small group game by giving each student ten markers (such as colored chips or cubes) and a paper with a circle on it. Each time the word card is read, the students place a marker in the circle if there is a rhyme.

- Students can extend the rhyme pattern by adding another rhyming word to the pair. This can be a whole-class or small-group activity.

- Read aloud a nursery rhyme (pages 173–176). Have the students march in place when they hear a pair of rhyming words.

mop shop	man pan
fun bun	sit kit
lip whip	pot dot

#50144 *Phonemic Awareness Activities & Games for Early Learners*

wet net	see knee
duck luck	ball small
rake lake	game same

eat meat	pest best
mill will	sand land
light right	sock rock

#50144   *Phonemic Awareness Activities & Games for Early Learners*

bank pan	can got
ball dot	hand feet
pluck sun	cake pain

Higglety Pigglety Pop

Skill:

Rhyming

Suggested Group Size:

Whole class or small group

Activity Overview:

Students will create rhyming patterns to use in a nursery rhyme.

Materials:

- "Higglety Pigglety Pop" (page 20)
- "Make-a-New-Rhyme Cards" (page 21)

Activity Preparation

1. Photocopy "Higglety Pigglety Pop" onto cardstock paper (or print copies from the CD).

2. Color the illustrations around the nursery rhyme and laminate for durability, if desired.

3. Photocopy "Make-a-New-Rhyme Cards" onto cardstock paper (or print copies from the CD).

4. Color and cut apart the cards.

5. Laminate the cards for durability, if desired.

Activity Procedure

1. Read "Higglety Pigglety Pop" slowly with the students several times.

2. Then, tell the students that on the next reading they are to clap their hands when they hear a rhyme. (For example, pop-mop, hurry-flurry.)

3. Explain to the students that you are now going to read the poem again. But this time you will use one of the rhyme cards to change the ending sounds to create a new rhyming pattern. For example, use the "Make-a-New-Rhyme Card" –ug and the rhyme becomes "Higglety, pigglety, pug, the dog has eaten the bug; the pig's in a hug, the cat's in a flug, higglety, pigglety, pug."

4. Allow the students to practice the new rhyming patterns by stopping the reading before you get to the ending sound, allowing the students to complete the rhyme pattern.

5. Continue with other "Make-a-New-Rhyme Cards." Shuffle the cards as necessary.

Adaptations

- Ask the students to suggest other things that the dog could have eaten to make even more fun rhymes.
- Using the "Make-a-New-Rhyme Cards," ask the students to say as many words as they can that end the same way.
- Ask the students to read (recite) their favorite version of the poem, pointing to the words as they read.

Higglety Pigglety Pop

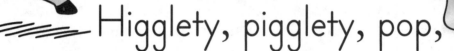

Higglety, pigglety, pop,
The dog has eaten the mop;
The pig's in a hurry,
The cat's in a flurry,
Higglety, pigglety, pop.

Make-a-New-Rhyme Cards

-ap	-en
-ill	-ug
-est	-ock

GO RHYME

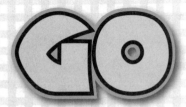

Skill:

Rhyming

Suggested Group Size:

4–6 students

Activity Overview:

Students will recognize rhyming words while playing a card game.

Materials:

- "Go Rhyme Picture Cards" (pages 24–29)

Activity Preparation

1. Photocopy "Go Rhyme Picture Cards" onto cardstock paper (or print copies from the CD).

2. Color and cut apart the cards.

3. Laminate the cards for durability, if desired.

Activity Procedure

1. Shuffle the picture cards and distribute evenly to the students.

2. Ask the students to hold the cards in their hands so only they can see the pictures.

3. Students will take turns asking one other student in the group if he or she has any picture cards that rhyme with one of the picture cards in their hands. For example: "Do you have any cards that rhyme with fish?"

4. If the student who was asked about the rhyme has a picture card that rhymes, then he or she says "yes," says the word, shows the card to the group, and gives it to the student who asked for the rhyme. The requesting student then puts the pair down in front of where he or she is sitting.

5. If the student says "no," the turn passes to the next student. This student then asks another student for a rhyming card.

6. The game continues until one student is out of cards.

7. Have all students read their rhyming cards to the group.

Adaptations

- Play the game with the whole class by giving one card to each student. Ask for a rhyme and have all the students with rhyming cards stand up.

- Play the game as a whole class and have student leaders.

- Use the cards to play rhyme match by turning them all upside down on a table. Students can take turns flipping the cards over two at a time to look for matches. If the student finds a rhyme match, he or she keeps the cards. The game continues until all the cards are matched up.

Go Rhyme Picture Cards

#50144   *Phonemic Awareness Activities & Games for Early Learners*

Go Rhyme Picture Cards (cont.)

Go Rhyme Picture Cards *(cont.)*

#50144   *Phonemic Awareness Activities & Games for Early Learners*   © Shell Education

Go Rhyme Picture Cards *(cont.)*

Funny Bunny

Skill:
Rhyming

Suggested Group Size:

Whole class or small group

Activity Overview:

Students will create rhyming nonsense words with a designated sound.

Materials:

■ "Funny Bunny Picture Cards" (pages 32–35)

Activity Preparation

1. Photocopy the "Funny Bunny Picture Cards" onto cardstock paper (or print copies from the CD).

2. Color and cut apart the cards.

3. Laminate the cards for durability, if desired.

Activity Procedure

1. Explain to the students that you will be playing a rhyming game called "Funny Bunny" using a super sound.

2. Select a sound that the class is working on to play "Funny Bunny." For example, if the super sound is /f/, the students will make words that rhyme with the cards that begin with /f/.

3. Hold up the picture cards one at a time. Have the students say the word that matches the picture, for example, *bunny*.

4. Have the students rhyme bunny with the super sound /f/ to make *funny*.

5. Continue with all the picture cards using the same super sound (dog-fog, hen-fen, etc.). Accept both real and nonsense words.

6. This activity can be used over and over with different super sounds.

Adaptations

- Select a blend or digraph as the super sound to begin the rhyme.
- Have the students name as many words as they can to rhyme with each picture card.
- Make sets of cards for the students to play the game independently at a learning center. Assign a letter of the alphabet to be the super sound.

Funny Bunny Picture Cards

Funny Bunny Picture Cards (cont.)

SYLLABLE SORT

Skill:

Syllable splitting

Suggested Group Size:

2–4 students

Activity Overview:

Students will sort picture cards based on the number of syllables in each word.

Materials:

- "Syllable Sort Picture Cards" (page 38–43)
- index cards or sticky notes

Activity Preparation

1. Photocopy the "Syllable Sort Picture Cards" onto cardstock paper (or print copies from the CD).

2. Color and cut apart the cards.

3. Laminate the cards for durability, if desired.

4. Write one number, 1, 2, or 3, on each of the index cards or sticky notes.

Activity Procedure

1. Place the number cards or sticky notes face up on a table. Have a small group of students sit around the table in order to sort the picture cards.

2. Shuffle the picture cards.

3. Draw one card at a time and show it to the students.

4. Ask the students to say aloud the word of the picture they see. Ask them to count the number of syllables in the word.

5. Students use choral response to say the word aloud and count the syllables.

6. Ask the students which number to place the card under and place the picture card under the correct index card or sticky note.

7. Continue sorting with remaining cards.

Adaptations

- Play the game with the students, allowing them to take individual turns for points.

- Photocopy the picture cards onto plain paper. Make enough for each student to have a picture. Cut along the lines, distribute the pictures, and have the students color them. Make class posters for one-, two-, and three-syllable words. Add other words to the posters as they come up in daily lessons or stories.

- Starting with the one-syllable words, have students select a card and write the sounds of the words on lined paper.

Syllable Sort Picture Cards

#50144   *Phonemic Awareness Activities & Games for Early Learners*   © *Shell Education*

Syllable Sort Picture Cards *(cont.)*

Clap, Snap, Tap

Skill:

Syllable splitting

Suggested Group Size:

Whole class

Activity Overview:

Students will practice counting syllables with the use of action cards.

Materials:

■ "Clap, Snap, Tap Action Cards" (pages 46– 47)

■ Word List (page 47)

Activity Preparation

1. Photocopy "Clap, Snap, Tap Action Cards" onto cardstock paper (or print copies from the CD).

2. Color and cut apart the cards.

3. Laminate the cards for durability, if desired.

4. Copy and laminate the word list for ease of use.

Activity Procedure

1. Display the action cards and practice each of the actions with the students. (Clapping, tapping one finger on the desk, and snapping fingers.)

2. Show the students how to count syllables with one action at a time.

3. Say a word from the list and model an action for each syllable. For example: "*cobweb - cob* (clap) *web* (clap)."

4. Ask the students, "How many syllables did you hear?" They should answer "Two," by counting the number of claps (or other actions).

5. Continue to practice the words in the word list, changing action cards as desired.

Adaptations

- Incorporate a pattern of actions for words. For example: Two-syllable words may be clap-tap. So the word *cobweb* would be *cob* (clap) *web* (tap).

- Challenge the students to think of words with many syllables, like *hippopotamus*. This could be turned into an adult involvement activity by encouraging students to learn words from family members.

- Add more challenging words to the word list as students become proficient with two- and three-syllable words.

Clap, Snap, Tap Action Cards

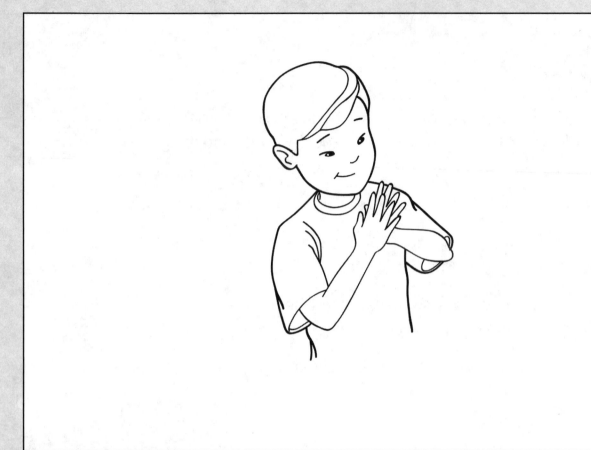

#50144   *Phonemic Awareness Activities & Games for Early Learners*

Two-Syllable Words		Three-Syllable Words	
basket	mailbox	basketball	magazine
birthday	napkin	beginning	microphone
finish	nutshell	butterfly	Saturday
habit	scarecrow	dangerous	telephone
lipstick	skateboard	gorilla	together
magnet	sunset	porcupine	tomorrow

Which One?

Skill:

Sound matching

Suggested Group Size:

Whole class or small group (2–5 students)

Activity Overview:

Students will identify a word that matches a designated sound from a group of words.

Materials:

- "Which One? Picture Cards" (pages 50–53)

Activity Preparation

1. Photocopy "Which One? Picture Cards" onto cardstock paper (or print copies from the CD).

2. Color and cut apart the cards.

3. Laminate the cards for durability, if desired.

4. If playing the game as a whole class, photocopy enough "Which One? Picture Cards" onto plain paper for each student in the class to have his or her own page.

Activity Procedure

1. Place a group of cards on the table so all the students in the group can see them. For example, cards of "dog," "snake," and "cat."

2. Say aloud the word that matches each picture.

3. Ask the students to identify a picture that begins with a designated sound. For example, "Which one begins with /s/?"

4. Students will use choral response naming snake.

5. Say, "Yes. *Ssssnake* begins with /s/."

6. Repeat with other picture cards and other sounds.

Adaptations

■ Copy enough picture cards for each student to sort independently. Repeat from #3 above, allowing the students to identify the pictures that match the sounds. Students will respond verbally and with picture sorting.

■ As a class, use an enlarged photocopy of the picture cards but do not cut them apart. Display the copy so the students can see the pictures. Students will point to the picture that matches the question: "Which one begins with _____?"

■ Read a nursery rhyme (pages 173–176). Using the "Which One? Picture Card" page, have students match sounds to words in the nursery rhyme.

Which One? Picture Cards

#50144   *Phonemic Awareness Activities & Games for Early Learners*

Which One? Picture Cards (cont.)

Sorting Bags

Skill:

Sound matching

Suggested Group Size:

2–5 students

Activity Overview:

Students will use sorting bags to match medial sounds of words.

Materials:

- "Sorting Bags Short Vowel Picture Cards" (pages 56–61)
- five paper lunch bags

Activity Preparation

1. Photocopy "Sorting Bags Short Vowel Picture Cards" onto cardstock paper (or print copies from the CD).

2. Color and cut apart the cards.

3. Laminate the cards for durability, if desired.

4. Write one vowel on each of the five bags with a marking pen.

5. Place one of the picture cards on the outside of the bag with the appropriate vowel. Keep the remaining picture cards for use during the game.

Activity Procedure

1. Select a Vowel Sorting Bag.

2. Explain to the students that they will be sorting the picture cards into the bag that matches the short vowel sound. Review the sound of the vowel on the bag you have selected.

3. Shuffle the cards and place them face down in front of you.

4. Select the cards one at a time and ask the students to tell you whether it belongs in the bag.

5. Continue drawing and sorting cards until the stack is all sorted.

6. Repeat the same procedure for other Vowel Sorting Bags.

Adaptations

- Play the game with a student leader. Ask the students to take turns sorting the picture cards.

- Place all Vowel Sorting Bags and all picture cards in a learning center. Students will sort the cards independently with their center group.

- Write a vowel on a blank piece of paper for each student in the group. Have the students draw pictures that have that short vowel sound in the middle.

Sorting Bags Short Vowel Picture Cards

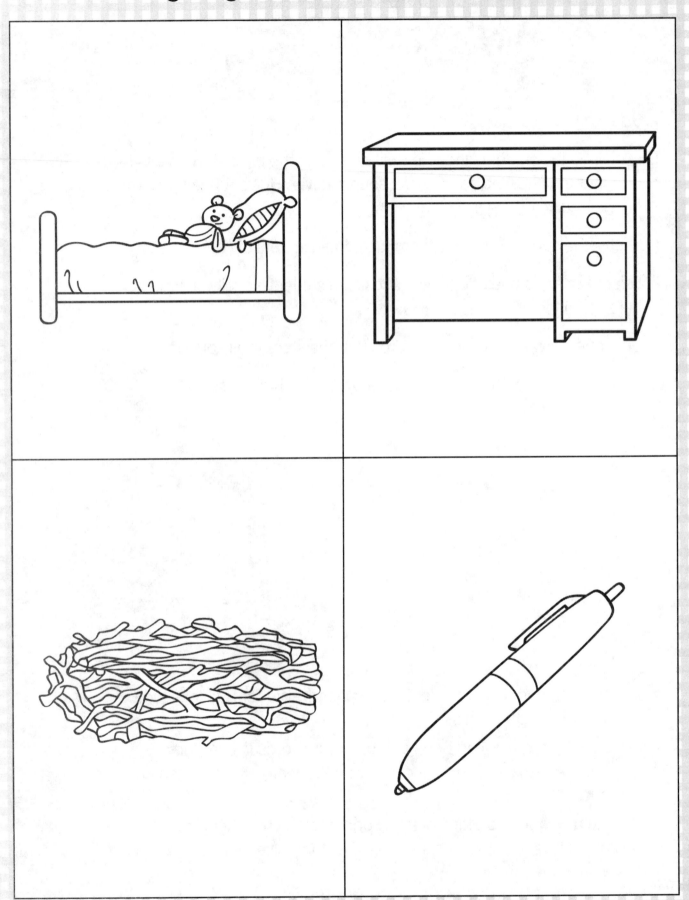

#50144   *Phonemic Awareness Activities & Games for Early Learners*

Sorting Bags Short Vowel Picture Cards *(cont.)*

#50144   *Phonemic Awareness Activities & Games for Early Learners*

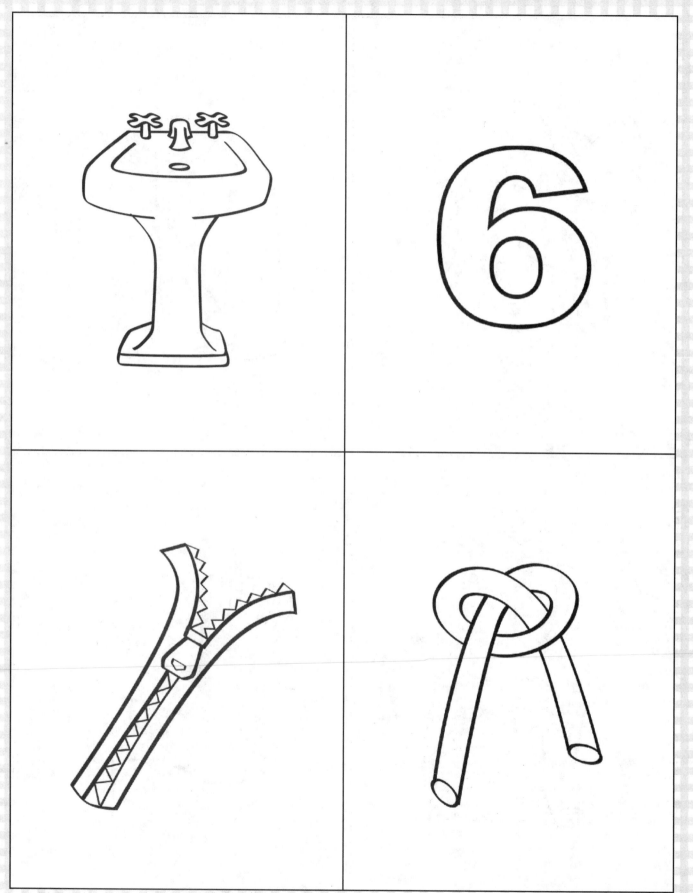

Sorting Bags Short Vowel Picture Cards *(cont.)*

#50144   *Phonemic Awareness Activities & Games for Early Learners*   © Shell Education

Sorting Bags Short Vowel Picture Cards *(cont.)*

Oh Yes!

Skill:

Sound matching

Suggested Group Size:

2–5 students

Activity Overview:

Students will identify whether words do or do not belong in a group of words.

Materials:

- "Oh Yes!/Oh No! Puppets" (pages 64–65)
- tongue depressors or paint sticks (two per child)
- glue

Activity Preparation

1. Photocopy the "Oh Yes!/Oh No! Puppets" onto cardstock paper (or print copies from the CD). Make enough copies so that each student in the group will receive one pair of puppets.

2. Color and cut out the puppets.

3. Laminate the puppets for durability, if desired.

4. Glue a craft stick to the bottom, backside of each puppet.

Activity Procedure

1. Give each student a pair of puppets.

2. Explain to the students that you are going to say three words.

3. If all the words begin with the same sound, the students will hold up the Oh Yes! puppet and say, "Ohhh Yes!"

4. If the words do not all begin with the same sound, the students will hold up the Oh No! puppet and say, "Ohhh Nooo!"

5. For example, for the words *pig, pet, pen*, students will say, "Oh Yes!" For the words *pig, net, pup*, students will say, "Oh No!"

6. Play the game with 10–15 groups of words.

Adaptations

- Play the game to match ending sounds of words.
- Play the game to match rhyming words.
- Photocopy enough puppets for each student to have a set. Glue them back-to-back on a tongue depressor or paint stick. All the students can respond during the game by flipping the puppet showing one side or the other.

Oh Yes! Puppet

#50144 *Phonemic Awareness Activities & Games for Early Learners*

Oh No! Puppet

Mystery Names

Skill:

Sound matching

Suggested Group Size:

Whole class

Activity Overview:

Students will identify a name that matches the target sound.

Materials:

- "Mystery Names Name Cards" (page 68)
- "Mystery Names Sentence Frames" (page 69), optional

Activity Preparation

1. Photocopy "Mystery Names Name Cards" onto cardstock paper (or print copies from the CD). Make enough name cards for each student to have his or her own.

2. Write the names of each student in the class on the Name Cards, one per card.

3. If using the "Mystery Names Sentence Frames," photocopy and cut apart. Make enough for each student to have his or her own frame.

#50144 *Phonemic Awareness Activities & Games for Early Learners*

Activity Procedure

1. Give each student the card with his or her name on it.

2. Tell the students: "I'm thinking of a name that starts with /j/. If your name starts with /j/ please stand up."

3. The students whose names begin with the sound /j/ will stand up.

4. Acknowledge the students' names. "Yes! Jason and Julie both begin with /j/."

5. Continue the game with different beginning sounds until all students have had a chance to stand up.

Adaptations

- Have the students perform an action that begins with the same letter as their names. For example, Jason and Julie could jump.

- Play the game allowing a student to be the leader and call out a sound.

- Play the game but focus on the ending sound. "I'm thinking of a name that ends with /n/. Yes! Jason and Evan end with /n/."

- Give one "Mystery Name Sentence Frame" to each student to write his or her name and a word that begins with the same letter.

Mystery Names Name Cards

#50144 *Phonemic Awareness Activities & Games for Early Learners*

Mystery Names Sentence Frames

My name is _____

I like _____

My name is _____

I like _____

Who Belongs?

Suggested Group Size:

Whole class

Activity Overview:

Students will listen to a group of words and identify a word that does not belong.

Materials:

- "Humpty Dumpty Nursery Rhyme" (page 72)
- "Who Belongs? Word Lists" (pages 73–75)

Activity Preparation

1. Photocopy "Humpty Dumpty Nursery Rhyme" onto cardstock paper (or print a copy from the CD).

2. Color the nursery rhyme illustration and laminate the card for durability, if desired.

3. Photocopy "Who Belongs? Word Lists" for ease of use.

4. Laminate the word lists for durability, if desired.

Activity Procedure

1. Read "Humpty Dumpty" with the students, emphasizing the rhyming words as you read.

2. Ask the students to identify the rhyming words in the nursery rhyme.

3. Tell the students to listen carefully as you read to them from the word lists. Tell them all the words in the lists are supposed to rhyme. Explain to the students that they are to listen for the word that DOES NOT belong (does not rhyme). Students answer using choral response.

4. Continue the activity with the other groups of words from the list.

Adaptations

■ Use the "Humpty Dumpty Nursery Rhyme" to make an overhead transparency. Using an overhead projector read the rhyme to the students and then say the rhyme together. Circle rhyming words with a colored pen.

■ Repeat the activity with other nursery rhymes (pages 173–176).

■ Reread "Humpty Dumpty," substituting another rhyming word for *wall*. For fun, try *ball*, *doll*, *mall*, and *stall*.

Humpty Dumpty

Humpty Dumpty
Sat on a wall,
Humpty Dumpty
Had a great fall;
All the king's horses
And all the kings men,
Couldn't put Humpty
Together again.

wall had fall	sat and mat
all ball not	den men to

had mad the	put men again
not bad cot	man soot put

#50144   *Phonemic Awareness Activities & Games for Early Learners*   © Shell Education

Who Belongs? Word Lists *(cont.)*

gone fawn and	on sad dad
hand and men	king all sing

Checkerboard Match

Skill:

Sound Matching

Suggested Group Size:

Small group
(2–4 students)

Activity Overview:

Students will identify a picture that matches a designated beginning letter sound.

Materials:

- "Checkerboard Match Game Board" (page 78)
- "Checkerboard Match Word List" (page 79)
- markers for checkerboard (counters, cubes, etc.)

Activity Preparation

1. Photocopy "Checkerboard Match Game Board" onto cardstock paper. Make enough copies for each student to have his or her own game board.

2. Laminate the game boards for durability.

3. Cut the checkerboards to size.

4. Photocopy "Checkerboard Match Word List" for ease of use. Laminate for durability, if desired.

Activity Procedure

1. Give each student in the group a checkerboard and a marker to move on the checkerboard. Review all of the pictures on the checkerboard with the students.

2. Explain to the students that the object of the game is to move their markers from the bottom of the checkerboard (the side closest to them) to the top of the checkerboard (the side furthest from them).

3. Tell the students to listen carefully to the beginning sound of the words you will say.

4. Once they hear and identify the beginning sound of the word, the students will move their markers on the board to a box with a picture that begins with the same sound as the word. For example, "The word is *tongue*. Move your marker to a box with a picture that begins with the same sound as *tongue*."

5. Students will move their markers to the appropriate box, such as to the box with the picture of the tiger.

6. Call out one word from each row on the word list. The words in each numbered row correspond with the checkerboard rows. (If desired, call out additional words from each row that begin with different sounds. Students will move horizontally along the board in addition to moving vertically.)

7. The game is over when the marker is moved off the top of the checkerboard.

Adaptations

- Mix up the words from the columns on the word list to make the game more challenging.

- Cut up one of the gameboards to use as a "word list" for students to take turns being the leader and calling out words for other students.

- Use the checkerboard to play Sound Match BINGO. Students place a marker on the square when there is a sound match called.

- Read a nursery rhyme (pages 173–176) and use the words from it to find sound matches on the checkerboard.

Checkerboard Match Game Board

1				
2				
3				
4				

#50144   *Phonemic Awareness Activities & Games for Early Learners*

Checkerboard Match Word List

4	rabbit rake ran red ribbon ring rip rock rope rug ruler run
	jacket jeans jelly jellybeans jet job jog jump
	tag tape teapot ten tent tip tire top tub turtle
	nail nap neck necklace needle nest net nine noodles not nut
3	sad said saw seal sell seven sick sign sink soap sun
	game gate get gift girl go gorilla grab grass guitar
	yacht yam yarn yawn yell yellow yes yet yolk
	quart quarter question quick quilt quit quiet quiz
2	hammer hand hat has heart hen hit horse hop hose
	wag watch water watermelon well wet win wing with worm
	magic mask maze miss mitten monkey mop moose mouse
	iguana ill in ink insect inside
1	baby ball bat bear bed bell big bike
	pan parrot pear pencil penguin pet pick pin pizza pop puppet
	deer desk dig dime doll donkey door duck
	keep key kid king kiss kit kite kitten

Hands Up

Skill:

Sound matching

Suggested Group Size:

Whole class

Activity Overview:

Students listen for a specific sound in a list of words and respond when they hear a sound that does not match.

Materials:

- "Hands Up Direction Cards" (page 82)
- "Hands Up Word List" (page 83)

Activity Preparation

1. Photocopy the "Hands Up Direction Cards" onto cardstock paper (or print copies from the CD).

2. Color and cut apart the cards.

3. Laminate the cards for durability, if desired.

4. Photocopy the "Hands Up Word List" for ease of use.

5. Laminate the word list for durability, if desired.

#50144 *Phonemic Awareness Activities & Games for Early Learners*

Activity Procedure

1. Place the cards where the students can see them.

2. Explain to the students you will say a list of words from the word list that begin with a specific sound of a letter of the alphabet. For example, the sound of letter /f/.

3. Tell students they will listen for the words that DO NOT begin with the specific sound you are looking for. If the sound is /f/, students will listen for words that do not begin with this sound.

4. Students will raise their hands when they hear a word that does not belong. Students will put their hands down when they hear a word that begins with the designated sound.

5. For example: if the list reads *fish, fin, fat, dig, fill, full, go, fog, fun*, students would raise their hands for *dig* and *go*. Hands are down for all words that begin with the /f/ sound.

6. Continue the activity using other beginning letter sounds from the word list.

Adaptations

- Play the game with a small group (2–4 students) to allow for assessment of the discernment of the sounds.

- As students become proficient, ask them to identify the letter that represents the sound. Have the students trace the letter with their finger on their desk or on the carpet. Speed up the calling of the words.

- Play the game changing the sound to listen for from the beginning to the ending sound or medial sound.

Hands Up Direction Cards

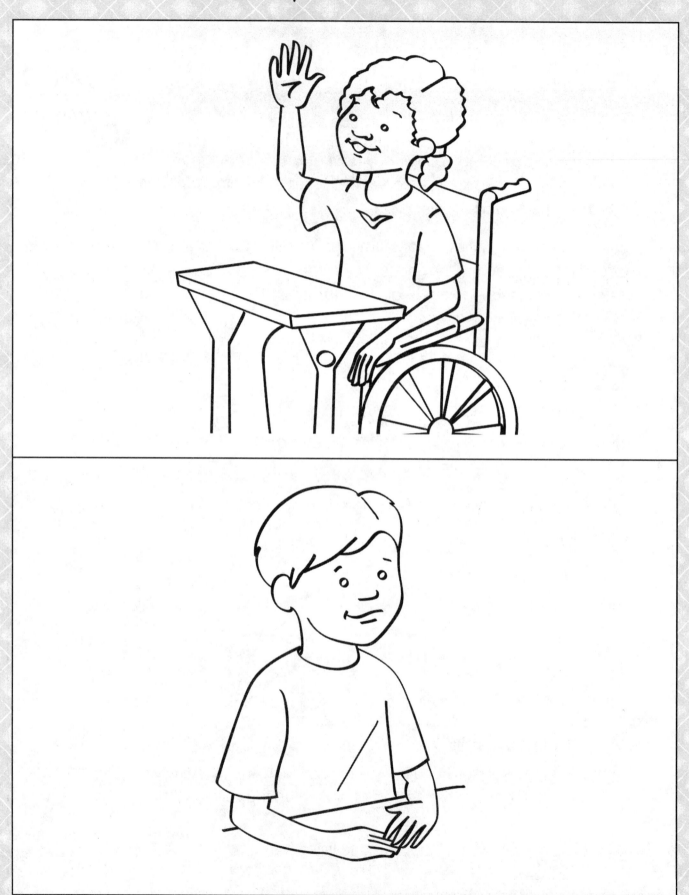

#50144   *Phonemic Awareness Activities & Games for Early Learners*

Hands Up Word List

Aa	alligator	anchor	ankle	ant	apple	astronaut
Bb	baby	ball	bat	bear	bed	bell
Cc	cage	cake	cap	cape	car	carrot
Dd	desk	dig	dime	dog	doll	door
Ee	egg	elbow	elephant	elevator	envelope	excellent
Ff	feather	fish	fence	foot	fork	fox
Gg	game	get	gift	girl	gorilla	grass
Hh	hammer	hat	heart	his	hop	horse
Ii	igloo	iguana	ill	ink	insect	inside
Jj	jacket	jar	jeans	jet	jog	jump
Kk	kangaroo	key	kid	kiss	kite	kitten
Ll	ladder	leaf	leg	let	lid	lion
Mm	man	mask	miss	monkey	moon	mop
Nn	nap	nail	necklace	nest	noodles	nose
Oo	octopus	off	office	olive	on	otter
Pp	pan	pear	pencil	pet	pick	pig
Qq	quarter	queen	question	quiet	quilt	quiz
Rr	rabbit	rake	ribbon	ring	rock	rug
Ss	saw	seal	sell	sign	sink	soap
Tt	tag	teapot	ten	tiger	tire	top
Uu	umbrella	umpire	under	up	upset	us
Vv	vacuum	valentine	van	vase	very	violin
Ww	wag	watch	well	wet	wing	worm
Xx	wax	mix	six	ox	box	fox
Yy	yacht	yarn	yawn	yes	yesterday	yo-yo
Zz	zag	zebra	zero	zipper	zoo	zoom

Little Boy Blue

Skill:

Sound isolation

Suggested Group Size:

Whole class

Activity Overview:

Students will practice the discernment of the beginning sounds of words.

Materials:

- "Little Boy Blue Nursery Rhyme" (page 86)
- "Little Boy Blue Color Picture Cards" (page 87)

Activity Preparation

1. Photocopy "Little Boy Blue Nursery Rhyme" onto cardstock paper (or print a copy from the CD).

2. Laminate for durability, if desired.

3. Photocopy "Little Boy Blue Color Picture Cards" onto cardstock paper (or print copies from the CD).

4. Color the pictures to reflect the colors or the beginning letter sounds you want children to focus on. For example, color the rabbit red, color the parrot purple, etc.

5. Cut apart the cards.

6. Laminate the cards for durability, if desired.

Activity Procedure

1. Read "Little Boy Blue" to students.

2. Ask the students which words in the rhyme begin with /b/? (*boy* and *blue*)

3. Ask the students if they have ever seen a blue boy. Show the picture card of the blue boy.

4. Show the students the other picture cards and ask the students to say the name of the color and the picture (such as purple parrot, red rabbit, etc.).

5. Show the students all the cards on the table. Ask the students which words begin with /r/? (*red* and *rabbit*)

6. Take turns practicing all of the sounds on the cards.

Adaptations

- Ask the students, "What other words begin with /b/?" Make a list of the words. Use the words to make a sentence such as, "The blue boy blows bubbles."

- Read "Fiddle Dee Dee" (page 173) aloud. Ask the students which words begin with /f/ or /d/.

- Photocopy the "Little Boy Blue Color Picture Cards," one card for each student. On the back of their card, students draw a picture that matches the beginning sound of the picture on the card.

Little Boy Blue

Little boy blue, come
blow your horn;
The sheep's in the
meadow, the cow's in
the corn.
Where's the little boy
who looks after the
sheep?
He's under a
haystack, fast asleep.

#50144   *Phonemic Awareness Activities & Games for Early Learners*

Little Boy Blue Color Picture Cards

boy

girl

rabbit

parrot

Vowel Puppets

Skill:

Sound isolation of medial sounds

Suggested Group Size:

2–6 students

Activity Overview:

Students will identify the medial sounds in words.

Materials:

- "Vowel Puppets" (pages 90–94)
- "Vowel Puppets CVC Word List" (page 95)
- tongue depressors
- glue

Activity Preparation

1. Photocopy "Vowel Puppets" onto cardstock paper (or print copies from the CD). You will need to make enough puppets for each student in your small group to have his or her own set of puppets.

2. Color the puppets and laminate for durability, if desired.

3. Cut out the puppets.

4. Glue a tongue depressor to the back of each puppet.

5. Photocopy "Vowel Puppets CVC Word List" for ease of use.

6. Laminate the word list for durability, if desired.

Activity Procedure

1. Give each student a set of vowel puppets.

2. Say the names of each puppet with students. Then review the medial (middle) sound of the name of each puppet. (For example, hold up the cat puppet and say, "/a/ is the middle sound in *cat*.")

3. Go around the group and have the students practice the medial sounds in the name of each puppet.

4. Then ask students to show you the puppet with a specific medial sound. For example: "Show me the puppet whose name has the /i/ sound in the middle."

5. Continue with each of the medial sounds.

Adaptations

- Say random words from the "Vowel Puppet CVC Word List" and have the students hold up the vowel puppet whose name has the same medial sound.

- Give a different vowel puppet to each of five students. Have these students stand in designated areas around the room. Pass out the short vowel picture cards (pages 166–167) from the activity "Big Bug," one to each remaining student in the class. Have these students sort themselves among the vowel puppets according to the medial sound in the name of the picture on their cards.

- Explain to the students that vowels also say their names (long vowel sound). Repeat activities isolating the long vowel sounds.

Vowel Puppets—Cat

#50144   *Phonemic Awareness Activities & Games for Early Learners*

Vowel Puppets—Hen *(cont.)*

Vowel Puppets—Duck *(cont.)*

Vowel Puppets CVC Word List

Short a	Short e	Short i	Short o	Short u
lad	bed	chill	dock	cub
mad	fed	fill	lock	hub
pad	led	pill	rock	rub
sad	red	dip	sock	sub
tad	wed	hip	on	tub
ham	bend	sip	hop	bug
jam	lend	tip	mop	dug
fan	mend	will	pop	hug
man	send	fit	top	jug
pan	tend	pit	cot	mug
ran	vend	sit	dot	rug
tan	bet	wit	hot	cup
bat	get	ditch	lot	pup
cat	met	pitch	not	bus
fat	set	rich	tot	fuss

Listen and Act

Skill:

Sound isolation of medial sounds

Suggested Group Size:

Whole class

Activity Overview:

Students will listen to a list of words and follow an action card when they hear the targeted sound.

Materials:

- "Listen and Act Action Cards" (pages 98–102)
- "Vowel Puppets CVC Word List" (page 95)
- "Rub-a-Dub-Dub Nursery Rhyme" (page 103)

Activity Preparation

1. Photocopy the "Listen and Act Action Cards" onto cardstock paper (or print copies from the CD).

2. Color and cut apart the cards.

3. Laminate the cards for durability, if desired.

4. Photocopy the "Vowel Puppets CVC Word List" for ease of use.

5. Laminate the word list for durability, if desired.

6. Photocopy the "Rub-a-Dub-Dub Nursery Rhyme" for ease of use.

7. Laminate the nursery rhyme for durability, if desired.

Activity Procedure

1. Ask the students to stand in an open area in the classroom or on the playground.

2. Display an action card and say the word designating the action (such as *jump*). Explain to the students that you will be reading from a list of words. Tell them they are to listen for words with the /u/ sound from the middle of the word *jump*.

3. Tell the students that when they hear a word with the middle sound /u/ like in *jump* (for example, the /u/ sound in *nut*) they are to follow the action card and JUMP!

4. Say random words from the word list slowly, enunciating the medial sound carefully. Be sure to include words with the designated medial sound, as well as other medial sounds.

5. Repeat the activity in different sessions using the other action cards and their respective medial sounds.

6. Use one action card only until the students are proficient at discerning the medial sounds.

Adaptations

■ Do the activity listed above with a small group focusing on the medial sound the students are learning.

■ As the students become proficient at the activity, add another action card to the game. Continue until students are listening for all five short vowel sounds during one game.

■ Instead of using the "CVC Word List," read aloud the "Rub-a-Dub-Dub" nursery rhyme. Use action cards appropriate for the students' proficiency level (i.e., one sound, two sounds, etc.).

Listen and Act Action Card—Pat

Listen and Act Action Card—Sit (cont.)

Rub-a-Dub-Dub

Rub-a-dub-dub,
Three men in a tub,
And who do you think they be?
The butcher, the baker,
The candlestick maker,
And all of them going to sea.

THE TURTLE AND THE HARES

Skill:

Sound blending

Suggested Group Size:

2–5 students

Activity Overview:

The leader says a word by pronouncing each sound separately and the students reply by saying the word quickly with all sounds blended.

Materials:

- "Turtle and Hares Cards" (page 106)
- "Turtle and Hares CVC Word List" (page 107)
- yarn, string, or roving

Activity Preparation

1. Photocopy "Turtle and Hares Cards" onto cardstock paper (or print copies from the CD). One "Turtle Card" is needed for the leader. Copy enough pages for each student in the group to have one "Hare Card."

2. Color and cut apart the cards.

3. Laminate the cards for durability, if desired.

4. Punch two holes at the top of each card.

5. Cut lengths of string long enough to make a necklace that fits over student's head. Tie one end of the string in each hole.

Activity Procedure

1. Distribute the "Hare Card" necklaces, one to each student. You wear the "Turtle Card" necklace.

2. Explain to the students that the turtle does things very slowly, even speaking. Model speaking slowly for the students. Say, "The turtle says /ffff/ /aaaa/ /ssss/ /tttt/."

3. Tell students that hares do things quickly, even speaking. Model speaking fast for the students. Say, "The hares say fast," very quickly.

4. Tell the students you are going to be the turtle and they will be the hares. Tell the students you will be speaking words very slowly. Their job is to listen and then repeat the word back to you, but quickly, like a hare.

5. Say a word from the word list sound by sound, very slowly.

6. Students will respond by saying the word quickly.

7. Continue the activity with additional words from the word list.

Adaptations

■ Read aloud *The Tortoise and the Hare: An Aesop Fable*, adapted by Janet Stevens. Read some of the words from the story slowly like the tortoise. Have the students repeat the words fast like the hare.

■ Exchange necklaces so that one of the students is the turtle. Repeat the game above.

■ Photocopy enough "Turtle Cards" to reverse the game.

Turtle and Hares Cards

#50144   *Phonemic Awareness Activities & Games for Early Learners*

Turtle and Hares CVC Word List

fail	seed	gum	cake	lot
ham	pail	tug	cot	fed
ban	man	duck	rub	tip
chin	top	pitch	tuck	meal
hop	jug	line	dip	sad
bug	sock	late	deal	bill
dock	need	van	lad	kit
deed	me	nap	fake	not
mail	bait	hum	bit	led
jam	pan	luck	dot	real
Dan	cap	rich	sub	tad
shin	mug	mine	hip	chill
mop	dine	wait	feel	pit
hug	gate	sap	mad	tot
lock	ran	sum	lake	red
feed	lap	cub	fit	seal
nail	bum	puck	hot	fill
Sam	rug	witch	tub	sit
fan	ditch	nine	bed	wed
win	fine	bake	sip	wheel
pop	hate	tap	heel	pill
dug	tan	hub	pad	wit
rock	map	fad	hit	will

© Shell Education   #50144   *Phonemic Awareness Activities & Games for Early Learners*

Simon Says

Skill:

Sound blending

Suggested Group Size:

2–5 students

Activity Overview:

Students will play a familiar game while practicing sound blending.

Materials:

- "Simon Says Cards" (pages 110–113)

Activity Preparation

1. Photocopy the "Simon Says Cards" onto cardstock paper.

2. Laminate for durability.

3. Cut cards apart.

#50144   *Phonemic Awareness Activities & Games for Early Learners*

Activity Procedure

1. Have the students stand in an open area in the classroom or playground.

2. Explain to students that they will play a special game of Simon Says. Be sure all students understand the rules for Simon Says.

3. Tell the students that in this special game, they need to repeat the word you say before they touch the body part named. For example, if you say, "Simon says, touch your /n/ pause /ō/ pause /z/," the students must say the word *nose* before they touch their noses.

4. Use the "Simon Says Cards" to help you pronounce the sounds of the body part named when playing Simon Says.

5. Continue the game by calling out the other body parts using the "Simon Says Cards."

Adaptations

- Play the game as a whole class. Have students use choral response.

- Say all the sounds in the sentence. Simon says /t/ pause /u/ pause /ch/ pause /y/ pause /ō/ pause /r/ pause /ch/ pause /i/ pause /n/.

- Have the students draw a picture of one of the "Simon Says Cards" and label it. Students can make their own game cards to play the game independently.

Simon Says Cards

head
/h/ /e/ /d/

nose
/n/ /ō/ /z/

eyes
/ī/ /z/

ears
/ē/ /r/ /z/

#50144 *Phonemic Awareness Activities & Games for Early Learners*

lips
/l/ /i/ /p/ /s/

chin
/ch/ /i/ /n/

hair
/h/ /a/ /r/

neck
/n/ /e/ /ck/

Simon Says Cards *(cont.)*

hand
/h/ /a/ /n/ /d/

elbow
/e/ /l/ /b/ /ō/

shoulder
/sh/ /ō/ /l/ /d/ /r/

knees
/n/ /ē/ /z/

#50144   *Phonemic Awareness Activities & Games for Early Learners*

hip

/h/ /i/ /p/

feet

/f/ /ē/ /t/

toes

/t/ /ō/ /z/

waist

/w/ /ā/ /s/ /t/

Secret Draw

cat

Skill:

Sound blending

Suggested Group Size:

Whole class

Activity Overview:

Students will listen to segmented words and draw a picture of the word.

Materials:

- "Secret Draw Activity Sheet" (page 116)
- "Secret Draw Word List" (page 117)

Activity Preparation

1. Photocopy "Secret Draw Activity Sheet" for each student (or print copies from the CD).

Activity Procedure

1. Give copies of the activity sheet and pencils to the students. Have the students write their names on the activity sheets or prepare each student's sheet with his or her name ahead of time.

2. Tell the students that you will be reading some words to them. Explain that you will pronounce the words one sound at a time. Ask the students to listen carefully to the word and to draw a quick picture of the word the sounds represent.

3. Say words from the word list one sound at a time, repeating the direction, such as "Listen and draw the secret word /c/ /a/ /t/." Be sure to pause for a few minutes between words to allow students sufficient time to draw.

4. Ask the students to keep their drawing secret for one minute. Then ask the students to reveal the word aloud and show their picture. This allows all students to respond with the correct answer at the same time.

5. Repeat the procedure, saying words one sound at a time until all the boxes on the recording sheets are filled.

Adaptations

- Students can color their secret draw pictures. Have students identify the beginning sounds of the words and write the letter in the square.

- Students use their pictures from the activity sheet to count the syllables in each word. Have the students write the number of syllables in the box next to their pictures.

- Cut apart a copy of "Secret Draw Activity Sheet." Make a class poster for each sound and glue the student's pictures on the appropriate poster.

Secret Draw Activity Sheet

Name _____

#50144   *Phonemic Awareness Activities & Games for Early Learners*

Secret Draw Word List

cat	/c/ /a/ /t/
hat	/h/ /a/ /t/
hand	/h/ /a/ /n/ /d/
pan	/p/ /a/ /n/
rabbit	/r/ /a/ /b/ /i/ /t/
bat	/b/ /a/ /t/
nest	/n/ /e/ /s/ /t/
bell	/b/ /e/ /l/
lemon	/l/ /e/ /m/ /o/ /n/
bed	/b/ /e/ /d/
tent	/t/ /e/ /n/ /t/
desk	/d/ /e/ /s/ /k/
pill	/p/ /i/ /l/
mitten	/m/ /i/ /t/ /e/ /n/
fish	/f/ /i/ /sh/
pig	/p/ /i/ /g/
window	/w/ /i/ /n/ /d/ /o/
wig	/w/ /i/ /g/
top	/t/ /o/ /p/
lock	/l/ /o/ /ck/
fox	/f/ /o/ /x/
box	/b/ /o/ /x/
pot	/p/ /o/ /t/
dot	/d/ /o/ /t/
cup	/c/ /u/ /p/
duck	/d/ /u/ /ck/
rug	/r/ /u/ /g/
nut	/n/ /u/ /t/
bug	/b/ /u/ /g/
gum	/g/ /u/ /m/

#50144   Phonemic Awareness Activities & Games for Early Learners

MARY HAD A LITTLE WORD

Skill:

Sound blending

Suggested Group Size:

Whole class

Activity Overview:

Students will listen to the sounds of a word and identify the word.

Materials:

- "Mary Had a Little Lamb Nursery Rhyme" (page 120)
- "Mary Had a Little Word Cloze Activity" (page 121)

Activity Preparation

1. Photocopy the "Mary Had a Little Lamb Nursery Rhyme" onto cardstock paper (or print copies from the CD).

2. Color the nursery rhyme illustration.

3. Laminate the nursery rhyme for durability, if desired.

4. Photocopy the "Mary Had a Little Word Cloze Activity" onto cardstock paper (or print copies from the CD).

5. Laminate for durability, if desired.

Activity Procedure

1. Say the nursery rhyme "Mary Had a Little Lamb" to the students. Then sing the rhyme.

2. Explain to the students that you will change the song by changing a word. Ask the students to guess what word Mary has.

3. Using "Mary Had a Little Word Cloze Activity," say or sing to the students, "Mary Had a Little Word that sounded just like this: /d/ /o/ /g/."

4. Continue reading or singing from the cloze activity: "Tell me, what's the word you hear? . . . etc. The word sounds just like this____!" Pause and signal to the students for a response. The response should be the word *dog*!

5. Say, "Dog! Yes! The word Mary has now is *dog*. Would you like to try another word?"

6. Repeat with one-syllable animal words such as *pig, goat, lamb, sheep, horse, cow,* and *bird.* Remember you will say the sounds, not the spelling. For example, *bird* would be said as /b/ /ûr/ /d/.

Adaptations

■ Use the activity with two-syllable words. Encourage the students to think of animals Mary might have, for example, a chicken, rooster, or lizard.

■ After some practice, switch the activity so you say the words and the students say the sounds.

■ Have the students draw one of the animals and sound out the letters to label the drawing. Phonetic spelling is the objective.

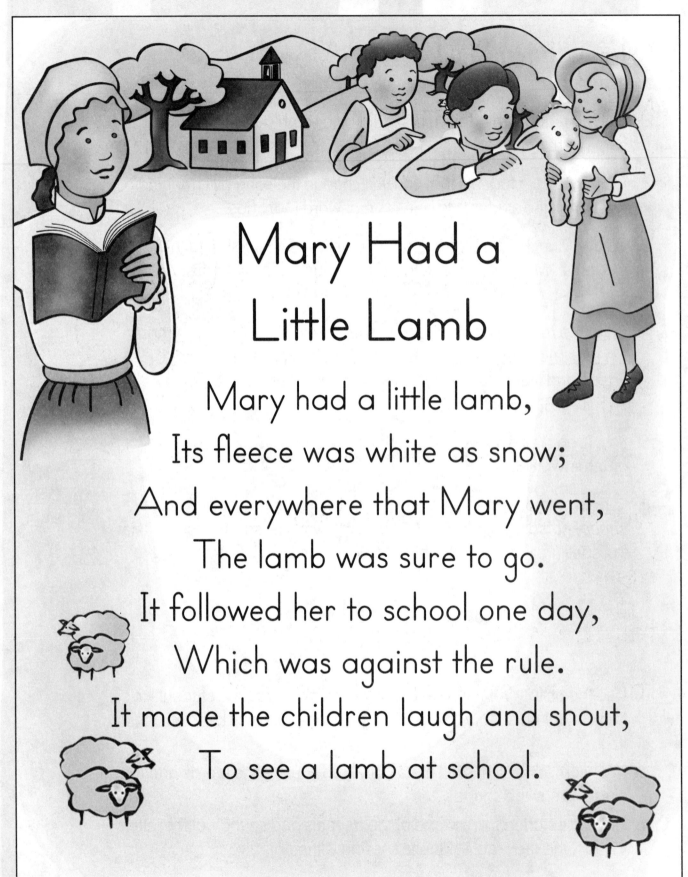

Mary Had a Little Lamb

Mary had a little lamb,

Its fleece was white as snow;

And everywhere that Mary went,

The lamb was sure to go.

It followed her to school one day,

Which was against the rule.

It made the children laugh and shout,

To see a lamb at school.

Mary Had a Little Word

Mary had a little word,

little word, little word,

Mary had a little word

that sounded just like this,

dog moon MAP frog pan

_____

Tell me what's the word

you hear,

word you hear, word you

hear,

tell me what's the word you hear,

the word sounds just like this!

_____. Yes!

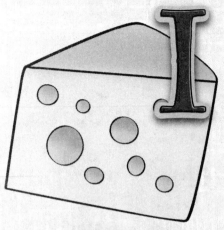

I Spy

Skill:

Sound blending

Suggested Group Size:

Whole class

Activity Overview:

Students will listen to words pronounced by sounds and respond by saying the words with the sounds blended.

Materials:

- "I Spy Picture Cards" (pages 124–125)

Activity Preparation

1. Photocopy the "I Spy Picture Cards" onto cardstock paper (or print copies from the CD).

2. Color and cut apart the cards.

3. Laminate the cards for durability, if desired.

Activity Procedure

1. Place the picture cards around the room to play the game *I Spy*.

2. Explain to the students that you will be looking around the room for items and saying the words of the items you are looking for, one sound at a time. Tell the students to listen carefully to the sounds of the word.

3. For example say, "I spy with my little eye… a /d/ /e/ /s/ /k/."

4. The students will respond individually or as a group, "desk" and point to the object or the I Spy picture card.

5. You may either use only the words from the "I Spy Picture Cards" or choose an object from inside the room.

6. Practice with at least eight words.

Adaptations

- Choose teams before you begin and have each team take turns responding after you say, "I spy with my little eye . . . ." Give each team a point for a correct answer.

- In a small group, lay out four cards and play *I Spy*. Call on students individually to say the word and identify the picture. Turn card over and replace with another card.

- Give the students blank index cards and have them draw a picture of an object. Use the new picture cards to play the game. Hint: The objects can come from a storybook the class is reading.

I Spy Picture Cards

wheel

/wh/ /ē/ /l/

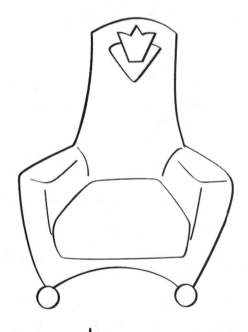

shark

/sh/ /ä/ /r/ /k/

cheese

/ch/ /ē/ /z/

throne

/th/ /r/ /ō/ /n/

#50144   *Phonemic Awareness Activities & Games for Early Learners*   © Shell Education

train

/t/ /r/ /ā/ /n/

spider

/s/ /p/ /ĭ/ /d/ /r/

snail

/s/ /n/ /ā/ /l/

star

/s/ /t/ /ä/ /r/

STRETCHY mitt WORDS

Skill:

Sound segmentation

Suggested Group Size:

Whole class

Activity Overview:

Students will verbally and kinesthetically segment the sounds in words.

Materials:

- "Stretchy Words Picture Cards" (pages 128–130)
- "Stretchy Words Action Cards" (page 131)

Activity Preparation

1. Photocopy "Stretchy Words Picture Cards" onto cardstock paper (or print copies from the CD).

2. Color and cut apart the cards.

3. Laminate the cards for durability, if desired.

4. Photocopy "Stretchy Words Action Cards" onto cardstock paper (or print copies from the CD).

5. Color and cut apart the cards.

6. Laminate the cards for durability, if desired.

#50144   *Phonemic Awareness Activities & Games for Early Learners*

Activity Procedure

1. Select an area in the classroom or outside where the students can move their bodies safely.

2. Show the students one of the action cards and demonstrate its movement. For *arms spread apart*, start with palms together in front of you and slowly move your hands apart until your arms are outstretched. For *hands in the air*, start by bending to touch your toes or ankles and then slowly raise your arms until they are raised high above your head. Have the students practice the action movements one time.

3. Explain to the students that you are going to be showing them pictures of words and saying the words very slowly. The students are to begin the chosen action, for example, "Stretch out your arms," as soon as you begin to say the word. They are to complete the action as you finish saying the word. Remind them that they will be doing the actions slowly and not quickly.

4. Before beginning, give students an example to be sure all students understand the directions. Show the students one of the picture cards and say the word slowly, such as "Bbbbbuuuuusssss." Model the chosen action as you say the word.

5. Repeat for five or six words.

Adaptations

- Students can put the word back together after the action is complete. After arms are outstretched for "bbbbbuuuuusssss," the students can say the word "bus" while clapping their hands together.

Stretchy Words Picture Cards

#50144 *Phonemic Awareness Activities & Games for Early Learners*

Stretchy Words Action Cards

Sound Boxes

Skill:

Sound segmentation

Suggested Group Size:

2–5 students

Activity Overview:

Students will listen to words and identify the number of sounds using Elkonin boxes.

Materials:

- "Sound Boxes Recording Sheet" (page 134)
- "Sound Boxes Word Lists" (page 135)
- markers (beans, counters, pennies, etc.)

Activity Preparation

1. Photocopy one "Sound Boxes Recording Sheet" for each student onto cardstock paper (or print copies from the CD).

2. Laminate "Sound Boxes Recording Sheets" for durability, if desired.

3. Photocopy the "Sound Boxes Word Lists" for ease of use.

4. Laminate the word list for durability, if desired.

5. Count out four markers for each student.

Activity Procedure

1. Give each student a Recording Sheet and four markers (beans, counters, pennies, etc.).

2. Explain to the students that you are going to read some words. They will listen for the number of sounds in the words. Students will slide their markers into one of the boxes on their recording sheets each time they hear a distinct sound in the word. For example, if a word has three sounds, students will slide in a marker for each of the three sounds they hear.

3. Begin with the two-sound words on the word list. Ask the students to place their index fingers on the picture of the circle on their recording sheets.

4. Ask the students to count how many boxes are next to the circle (2). Tell the students they will use these boxes for their markers when listening for the sounds.

5. Say a two-sound word from the word list. For example: "aaaatttt." Model for the students how to move a marker into the box when they hear each of the sounds.

6. Repeat with as many two-sound words as needed before moving to words with three or four sounds.

Adaptations

- Have a student leader use the picture cards from "Stretchy Words" (pages 128–130) to say words slowly for other students to identify the sounds. Students may use tally marks to count the sounds.

- Use overhead pens on the laminated recording sheets to write the letters that represent the sounds in the words.

Sound Boxes Recording Sheet

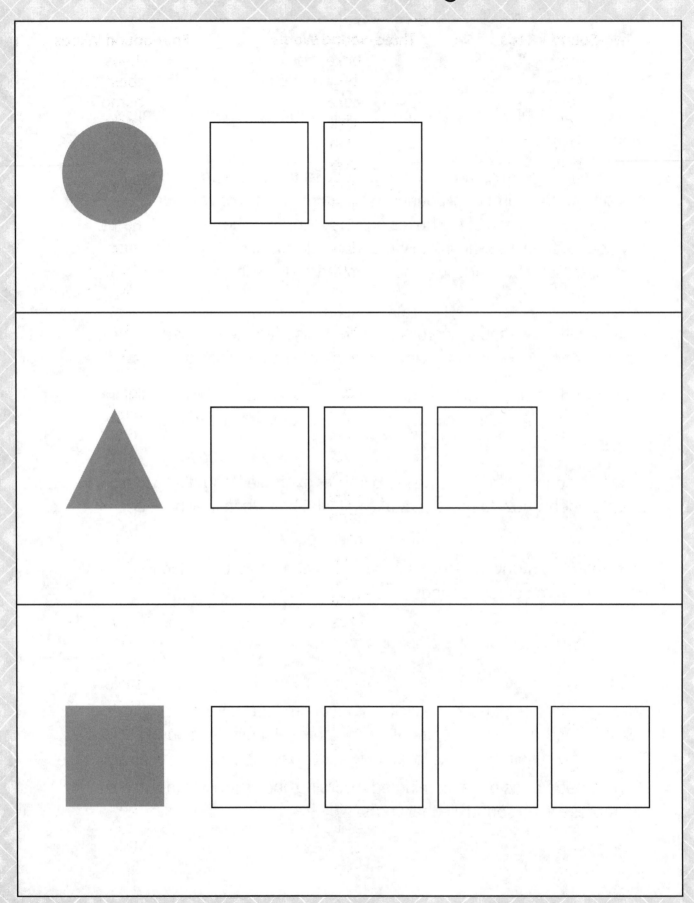

Sound Boxes Word Lists

Two-Sound Words	Three-Sound Words	Four-Sound Words
am	bake	beds
an	bug	best
as	cake	bump
at	chill	camp
bee	chin	cats
bow	cub	club
bye	dock	drop
day	duck	drug
do	fail	drum
eat	fan	fans
go	feed	flag
hay	feel	flat
hi	fill	fled
in	fine	flip
it	gate	great
lie	ham	hens
low	jam	lamp
may	lake	maps
me	line	nest
my	lock	pans
no	luck	pink
oak	mad	plate
on	man	ramp
pay	meal	skin
pea	mine	skit
pie	nail	slam
ray	nine	sled
row	pail	slid
say	pan	slip
see	pill	slit
sew	ran	smile
show	rich	snag
tea	sad	speak
tie	seal	spill
toe	seed	spin
two	tad	stone
up	tan	stop
us	van	train
way	wait	trip
we	will	vest

Roll the Sound

nail

dime

cake

Skill:

Sound segmentation

Suggested Group Size:

2–4 students

Activity Overview:

Students will say the sounds of a word as a ball rolls from student to student.

Materials:

- "Roll the Sound Picture Cards" (pages 138–141)
- playground ball or beach ball

Activity Preparation

1. Photocopy "Roll the Sound Picture Cards" onto cardstock paper (or print copies from the CD).

2. Color and cut apart the cards.

3. Laminate the cards for durability, if desired.

4. Provide students in the group with a ball to roll to each other.

Activity Procedure

1. Students will sit on the floor in a circle three to four feet away from each other.

2. Explain to the students that they will be practicing the different sounds in words while they roll a ball to one another.

3. Shuffle the picture cards and place them face down in a stack.

4. The first student will pick a card and show it to the group. All the students will say the word together. For example, if the picture on the card is a ball, the students will all say, "ball."

5. The student who selected the card will begin rolling the ball to another student in the group, saying the first sound in the word and will continue saying the sound until the ball reaches the next student: "/bbbbbbbbb/."

6. The next student receives the ball and rolls it, says the second sound in the word as he or she in turn rolls it to the next student: "/oooooooo/."

7. The next student receives the ball and when he rolls it, he says the last sound, "/lllllllll/," as he rolls it to the last student.

8. As the last student receives the ball, all the students say the word: "ball."

9. Repeat by allowing another student to draw a picture word from the stack of picture cards.

Adaptations

■ Students can identify the letter of the alphabet that represents each sound after each round of Roll the Sound.

Roll the Sound Picture Cards

#50144   *Phonemic Awareness Activities & Games for Early Learners*

Roll the Sound Picture Cards (cont.)

Play Dough Stretch

Skill:
Sound segmentation

Suggested Group Size:

2–5 students

Activity Overview:

Students will stretch the sounds in words as they roll play dough.

Materials:

- "Play Dough Recipe" (page 144)
- "Play Dough Stretch Word List" (page 145)
- zip-top plastic bags

Activity Preparation

1. Prepare the dough according to the recipe.

2. Place dough in zip-top bags to preserve for repeated uses.

3. Photocopy "Play Dough Stretch Word List" for ease of use.

4. Laminate the word list for durability, if desired.

Activity Procedure

1. Give each student a bag with a small portion of play dough.

2. Demonstrate how to roll the play dough on the table to form a "hot dog." (Roll it into a ball first and then have the students roll with four fingers on the table applying gentle pressure.)

3. Let the students try rolling the play dough into a hot dog and then squeezing it back into a ball.

4. Tell the students they will practice stretching words by their sounds like they are stretching their play dough.

5. Say a word, for example, *play*. Tell the students to begin rolling the play dough as they say the sounds of the word: "/pppppppp/ /lllllll/ /aaaaaaa/."

6. Stop rolling when you finish the sounds.

7. As the students squeeze the play dough back into a ball, have them say the word again as a group: "play."

8. Repeat with other words from the word list.

Adaptations

- Roll the play dough into a hot dog shape. As the students say the sounds, they separate the hot dog into pieces, one piece for each sound. Say the sounds and push the pieces back together. Say the word again.

- Roll the play dough into a hot dog shape and flatten it. After the students say the sounds of the word, they use a toothpick or pencil to etch the letters in the play dough.

- Roll the play dough into a hot dog shape. As you say the word slowly, have the students indent the play dough with their finger one time for each sound. Have them count the number of sounds in the word.

Play Dough Recipe

Ingredients

3 cups flour

1½ cups salt

3 cups water

2 tbsp. vegetable oil

1 tbsp. cream of tartar

1 package "Powdered Drink"

a few drops food coloring

Directions for Preparation

Mix all of the ingredients in a large saucepan. Cook over medium–low heat, until the dough comes away from the edges of the pan and it becomes difficult to move the spoon. Remove from heat. Cool until it can be handled. Place on counter or wax paper and knead 3–4 times. Store in an air–tight container or plastic zipper bag.

Play Dough Stretch Word List

beach	glide	skate
beam	grave	slide
bike	hoop	slope
bite	kite	snake
blade	late	sole
blue	leaf	soon
boom	lean	speak
boot	like	spine
booth	male	spite
bride	mean	spoon
broke	mine	state
cake	moon	steam
chime	mute	stone
clear	note	stream
clue	pane	strike
cream	pave	stripe
cute	peach	suit
deal	pike	tape
dine	plane	teach
drove	plate	tile
each	prize	tone
eat	quite	tooth
fate	ripe	trade
five	safe	waste
fake	scoop	white
froze	shake	wide
gaze	shame	zoo

#50144   *Phonemic Awareness Activities & Games for Early Learners*

I Can Say

Skill:

Sound segmentation and sound blending

Suggested Group Size:

Whole class or small group

Activity Overview:

Students will segment and blend the sounds of a CVC word by using a familiar tune.

Materials:

- " 'I Can Say' Song Frame" (page 148)
- "CVC Word Family List" (page 149)

Activity Preparation

1. Photocopy the " 'I Can Say' Song Frame" onto an overhead transparency or onto cardstock paper, depending on how it will be used.

2. If using the song frame on cardstock, color and laminate for durability.

3. Photocopy the "CVC Word Family List."

4. Laminate the word list for durability, if desired.

Activity Procedure

1. Place the " 'I Can Say' Song Frame" where the students can see it.

2. Sing the song for the students to the tune of "Are You Sleeping? (Frere Jacques)." Have the students join in the singing.

3. Tell the students you will substitute a different word for the word *cat* in the song. Ask the students to sing along and tell you the sounds of the substituted word.

4. Use CVC words in word families from the word list to assist the students in identifying the sounds. For example, *cat, hat, bat, fat, mat, sat,* etc.

5. After the students have practiced one word family to proficiency, choose another from the word list.

Adaptations

■ Copy the " 'I Can Say' Song Frame" and cut it into sentence strips leaving off the CVC word. Using index cards or sentence strip pieces, draw simple pictures or write a CVC word to insert into the song. Students can choose a card to insert in the song and practice in small groups. This activity can be adult-directed or used as an independent learning center activity.

■ After practicing a group of words, you can model the spelling of the words. Give the students lined paper and have them practice writing the words. Use a highlighter to write the words for the students having difficulty forming the letters. Students can trace over the highlighted words.

■ Use the song to practice the sounds and letter names of spelling or vocabulary words the students are learning.

"I Can Say"
(sung to the tune of
"Frere Jacques")

I can say cat.

I can say cat.

/c/ /a/ /t/, /c/ /a/ /t/

Listen to the sounds I say.

Listen to the sounds I say.

/c/ /a/ /t/ CAT

/c/ /a/ /t/ CAT

CVC Word Family List

ban	can	fan	an	pan	ran	tan	van
cap	gap	lap	map	nap	sap	tap	zap
cane	gain	main	pain	rain	sane	vain	wane
bait	date	fate	gate	hate	late	mate	rate
bell	fell	sell	tell	well	yell		
bet	get	jet	let	met	net	pet	set
beat	feet	heat	meat	neat	seat		
bit	fit	hit	lit	pit	quit	sit	wit
hide	ride	side	tide	wide			
dine	fine	line	mine	nine	pine	vine	wine
bop	cop	hop	lop	mop	pop	sop	top
core	door	for	more	poor	sore	tore	wore
bought	dot	fought	got	hot	lot	not	pot
bug	dug	hug	jug	lug	mug	rug	tug
bun	done	fun	pun	run	sun	ton	won

Riddles

Skill:

Sound manipulation of beginning sounds

Suggested Group Size:

2–5 students

Activity Overview:

Students will listen to riddles and substitute the beginning sounds of words to make new words.

Materials:

- "Riddles Rime Word List" (page 152)
- "Riddles Blends and Digraphs Cards" (page 153)

Activity Preparation

1. Photocopy "Riddles Blends and Digraphs Cards" onto cardstock paper (or print copies from the CD).

2. Cut apart the cards.

3. Laminate the cards for durability, if desired.

4. Photocopy the "Riddles Rime Word List" for ease of use.

5. Laminate for durability, if desired.

Activity Procedure

1. Shuffle the cards. In a small group, explain to the students that they will answer riddles by changing the beginning sounds of words to make new words.

2. Select a card from the stack. Say to the students, for example, "Answer me this—What rhymes with *man*, but begins with /pl/?" The answer is *plan*.

3. For the word pattern in the riddle, use the word list. For the replacement sound in the riddle, select a card from the blends and digraph cards.

4. Ask the students if the new word is a real or nonsense word.

5. Repeat the riddle, selecting a new card from the stack.

Adaptations

- Play the game by dividing up the cards between the members of the group. Each student will answer his or her own riddle by holding up a card from his or her stack for the teacher to use in the riddle.

- When the students are proficient at beginning sound substitution, ask the riddle substituting the ending sound. For example, "What word will I have if I say *man* with a /p/ at the end?" The answer is *map*.

- Ask the riddle using a substitution for the medial sound. "What word will I have if I say '*wig*' with an /a/ in the middle?" The answer is *wag*.

Riddles Rime Word List

–ack	–ick
–ake	–ight
–ale	–ill
–all	–in
–ame	–ing
–ank	–ink
–ash	–ip
–at	–ir
–aw	–ock
–ay	–oke
–est	–ump
–ice	–unk

#50144   *Phonemic Awareness Activities & Games for Early Learners*   © Shell Education

Riddles Blends and Digraphs Cards

sh	ch
wh	sk
st	fl
pl	dr

Button Slide

Skill:

Sound manipulation with adding a sound

Suggested Group Size:

2–5 students

Activity Overview:

Students will add a sound to a word to make a new word.

Materials:

- "Button Slide Button Patterns" (page 156)
- "Button Slide Add-a-Sound Word List" (page 157)
- yarn, string, or roving

Activity Preparation

1. Photocopy "Button Slide Button Patterns" onto colored cardstock paper (or print copies from the CD). Copy enough for each student in the group to have five buttons.

2. Cut out buttons.

3. Laminate the buttons for durability, if desired.

4. Use a hole-punch to make the buttonholes.

5. Cut yarn in 18-inch pieces.

6. Thread five buttons onto each piece of yarn to create button slides.

7. Photocopy "Button Slide Add-a-Sound Word List" for ease of use.

8. Laminate the word list for durability, if desired.

Activity Procedure

1. Give each student in the group a "Button Slide" with the buttons all on the left side of the yarn.

2. Explain to the students that you are going to be saying some words to them. They are to listen for each sound in the word. Tell them that they will slide one button to the middle of the yarn for each sound they hear.

3. Choose a word from the word list and say the word slowly. Then repeat the word and as you say the sounds, count the sounds. For example, say "*Lack.* /l/ /a/ /ck/. 3 sounds."

4. Students will slide three buttons to the middle. (The extra buttons will be on the left.)

5. Say the word again. Students will touch a button for each sound in order, left to right, and then say the word again. "*Lack,* /l/ /a/ /ck/, *lack.*"

6. Tell the students you will make a new word by adding a sound to the beginning of the word. Slide a button from the left to the front of the other three buttons, saying /b/.

7. Say all the sounds together, touching each button from left to right to say the new word "/b/ /l/ /a/ /ck/, black."

8. Repeat with other words from the word list.

Adaptations

- Delete a sound. Say the larger word and touch the buttons to correspond with the sounds /b/ /l/ /a/ /ck/. Slide the first button to the left. Say the new word, touching the buttons for each sound /l/ /a/ /ck/.

Button Slide Button Patterns

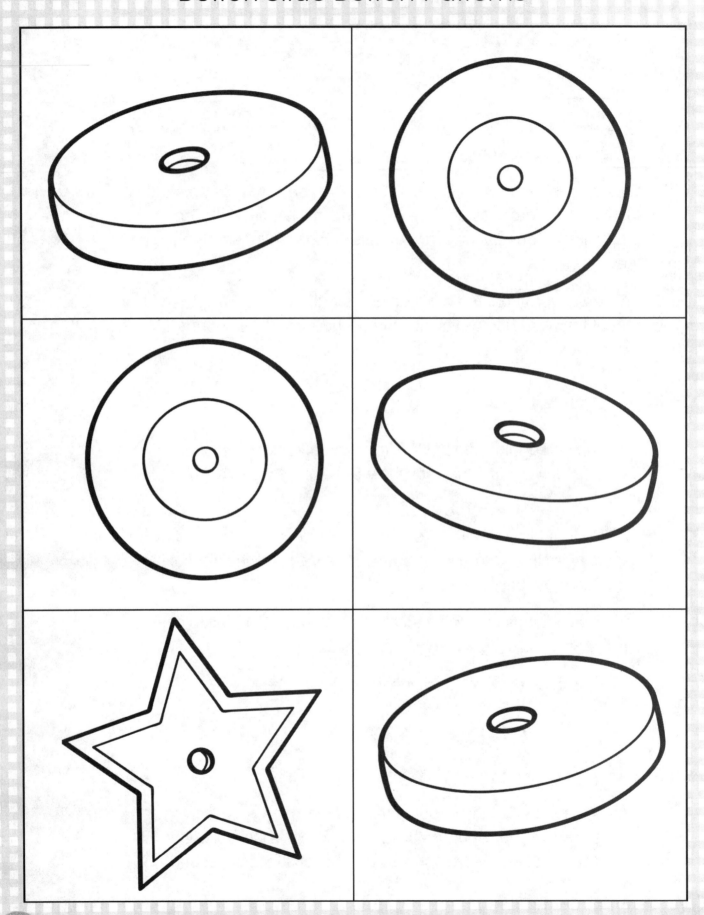

#50144   *Phonemic Awareness Activities & Games for Early Learners*   © *Shell Education*

Button Slide Add-a-Sound Word List

key	ski	mash	smash	reap	creep
kid	skid	nag	snag	ride	bride
kin	skin	nail	snail	right	bright
kit	skit	nap	snap	rim	trim
knees	sneeze	no	snow	rip	trip
lack	black	peak	speak	rise	prize
lamb	slam	pill	spill	roll	troll
lame	flame	pin	spin	rot	trot
lamp	clamp	poke	spoke	row	grow
lane	plane	rack	track	rug	drug
lap	clap	raft	draft	rum	drum
lass	glass	rag	brag	tack	stack
lay	clay	raid	braid	tale	stale
led	sled	rail	trail	team	steam
lend	blend	rain	crane	tick	stick
lick	slick	rake	brake	till	still
lid	slid	ramp	cramp	top	stop
lip	slip	rap	trap	tore	store
lit	slit	rash	crash	tuck	stuck
locks	blocks	rave	crave	wag	swag
lore	floor	ray	pray	way	sway
lot	plot	read	bread	weep	sweep
low	blow	read	tread	well	swell
lump	plump	ream	dream	wet	sweat

Tap, Tap, Run

Skill:

Sound manipulation by substituting a sound

Suggested Group Size:

10–12 students

Activity Overview:

Students will practice sound substitution using the first sounds in their names.

Materials:

- "Name Tent Card" (page 162)

Activity Preparation

1. Photocopy "Name Tent Card" onto cardstock paper (one for each student).

2. Write each student's name clearly on the "Name Tent Card."

Activity Procedure

1. Have the students sit in a large circle on the playground or carpet. Distribute "Name Tent Card" to the students and ask them to place their cards in front of them.

2. Each student will say the first sound of his or her name. Continue around the circle, so all students say the first sound of their names.

3. Choose one student to start. The first child walks around the outside of the circle tapping each child on the shoulder with two fingers, saying "tap."

4. When the student chooses, he or she says "run" as he or she touches another student's shoulder. Then, the student runs back to the empty space with his or her name.

5. The student who was tapped to run now takes a turn tapping and running. This time around, the student substitutes the first sound in his or her name for the /t/ in *tap* and the /r/ in *run*. So, Mary would say "map, map, map, mun!" Note: This game is similar to Duck, Duck, Goose except no one is "it" and no one gets "out."

6. Continue the game until all the children have had an opportunity to practice substituting beginning sounds.

Adaptations

- Use the "Riddles Blends and Digraphs Cards" (page 153) and call the sound substitution as the new student is chosen.

- Use the sounds of the student's first name to substitute the last sound in tap, tap, run to make nonsense words (i.e., Mary says "tam, tam, rum.").

Name Change

Alison

Skill:

Sound manipulation by substitution

Suggested Group Size:

4–5 students

Activity Overview:

Students will use the beginning sound of the names of their classmates to practice sound manipulation.

Materials:

- "Name Tent Card" (page 162)
- "Hey Diddle Diddle Nursery Rhyme" (page 163)
- tape or glue

Activity Preparation

1. Photocopy "Name Tent Card" on cardstock paper (or print copies from the CD). Make enough copies for each student to have his or her own name tent.

2. Laminate the cards for durability, if desired.

3. Write a student's name on each card.

4. Fold on dotted lines.

5. Photocopy "Hey Diddle Diddle Nursery Rhyme" for ease of use.

6. Laminate the nursery rhyme card for durability, if desired.

Activity Procedure

1. Give each student his or her "Name Tent Card" to place in front of him or her on the table.

2. Have each student say his or her name and show the name card to the other students in the group.

3. Choose a beginning sound from one of the students' names and say "Jason's name begins with /j/. Let's change all our names to begin with /j/."

4. Go around the group and say each child's name with the new sound. For example: Scott-Jott, Alison-Jalison, Cassie-Jassie.

5. Go around one more time asking the students in the group to say the names with the new sound.

6. Repeat using the beginning sound from each of the students' names in the group.

Adaptations

- Repeat activity as a whole class. Have the students sit in a big circle on the floor and place their name tent card in front of them.

- Use the "Hey Diddle Diddle Nursery Rhyme" to manipulate sounds. Change all words that begin with /d/ to the first sound of a student's name. For the name *Jessie, Hey Diddle Diddle* would become *Hey Jiddle Jiddle.*

- Use other nursery rhymes (pages 173–176) to repeat the game.

Name Tent Card

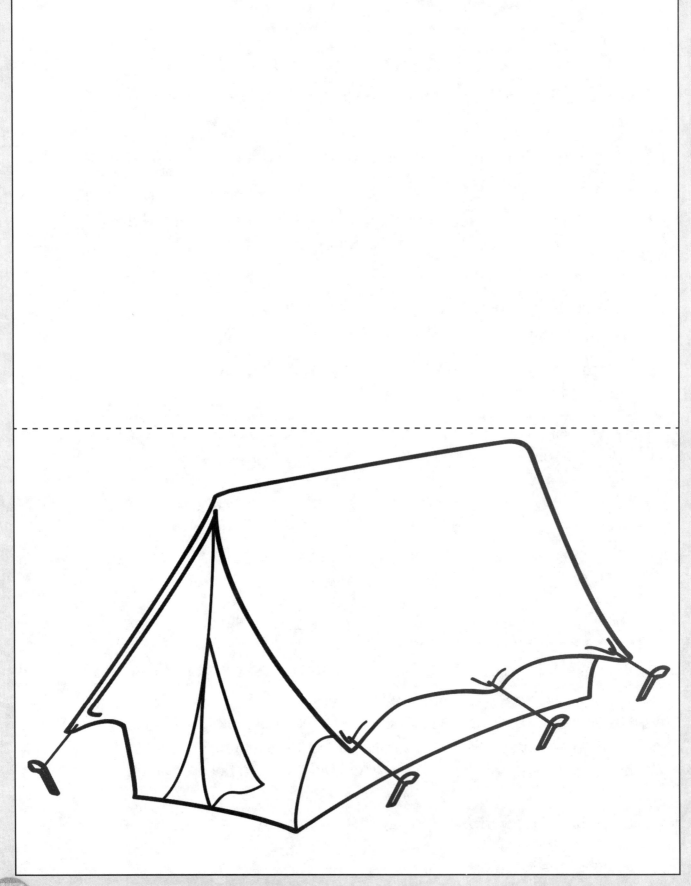

Hey Diddle Diddle

Hey diddle diddle,

The cat and the fiddle,

The cow jumped over

the moon;

The little dog laughed

to see such fun,

And the dish ran away

with the spoon.

Big Bug

bug

Skill:

Sound manipulation by substituting the medial sound

Suggested Group Size:

2–5 students

Activity Overview:

Students will substitute the medial sound in words using short vowel sounds.

Materials:

- "Short Vowel Picture Cards" (pages 166–167)
- "Short Vowel Word List" (page 167)

Activity Preparation

1. Photocopy "Short Vowel Picture Cards" onto cardstock paper (or print copies from the CD).

2. Color and cut apart the cards.

3. Laminate the cards for durability, if desired.

4. Photocopy "Short Vowel Word List" for ease of use. Laminate if desired.

Activity Procedure

1. In a small group, explain to the students that you can change a word by changing its middle sound.

2. Model by showing the picture card of the umbrella. Say, "This is an umbrella. It begins with /u/." Tell the students they are going to use the /u/ sound in *umbrella* to make a new word. Explain that by changing the middle sound in a word, a new word is made.

3. Say the word *big*. Now change the /i/ to /u/. /bbbb/ /iiiiii/ /gggg/ to /bbbb/ /uuuu/ /gggg/. *Bug. Big. Bug.*

4. Continue to use the short /u/ to substitute medial sounds using the word list.

5. Remind the students that the new words could be real or nonsense words.

Adaptations

- Give each student in the group a "Short Vowel Picture Card." Say a word from the "Short Vowel Word List." Each student will substitute the sound from his or her card to make a new word, for example, *big, bug, beg, bag, bog.* After several rounds, collect the picture cards, shuffle, and redistribute to the group. *(Optional:* You may want to give each student a chance to make a new card for his or her new word using the make your own card template.*)*

- Fold a blank paper in half twice to form four rectangles. Select words from the "Short Vowel Word List" to make silly phrases like *big bug* (mad/mud, pat/pet, fan/fin, sit/sat, bull/bell, fix/fox, Rick/rock, etc.). Students will draw pictures in each of the rectangles on the paper to represent the silly phrases.

- Play the game. Have the students "write" the vowel in the air, on the desk, or on the carpet with their index fingers.

Short Vowel Picture Cards

apple

egg

igloo

octopus

#50144   *Phonemic Awareness Activities & Games for Early Learners*

umbrella

Make your own card.

Short Vowel Word List

bat	get	dish	box	bus
can	bed	fish	cot	cup
dad	desk	gift	doll	duck
fan	head	jig	fox	dug
hammer	jet	kitten	got	mud
jacket	leg	lift	hop	nut
lamp	nest	pig	knot	puppet
mask	pen	sing	lock	run
rabbit	red	sit	mop	sun
sat	ten	wig	pot	tug
tag	vest	win	romp	tummy
wag	wet	zig	stop	tunnel
yam	yell	zipper	top	up

MAGIC WORD

log   lock   dig   dog

Skill:

Sound manipulation by sound substitution

Suggested Group Size:

Whole class

Activity Overview:

Students will create a new word by substituting a sound in any position in a word.

Materials:

- "Magic Word Change Song" (page 170)
- "Magic Word List" (page 171)

Activity Preparation

1. Photocopy "Magic Word Change Song" on cardstock paper for ease of use.

2. Laminate the song card for durability, if desired.

3. Photocopy the "Magic Word List" on cardstock paper for ease of use.

4. Laminate the word list for durability, if desired.

Activity Procedure

1. Explain to the students that they will play a game where they change one word into another word, one sound at a time, like magic.

2. Choose a word from the word list. For example, say, "We can change the word *man* into *cup*."

3. Sing the "Change Song" with the students. Then say, "What is *man* with /p/ at the end?" (map)

4. Sing the "Change Song" with the students. Then say, "What is *map* with /c/ at the beginning?" (cap)

5. Sing the "Change Song" with the students. Then say, "What is *cap* with /u/ in the middle? (cup). Yes, that's the Magic Word."

6. Continue to make magical new words by using new words from the word list and singing the "Change Song" with the students.

Adaptations

- Give each student a paper or index card with three boxes drawn on it side-by-side and one marker (bean, cube, button, penny, etc.). Each time you change a sound in a word, have the student slide the marker into the appropriate box (i.e., if you change the middle sound, the student moves a marker into the middle box).

- Write the word in large print on a whiteboard. Quickly erase the letter (sound) that is changing and write the new letter (sound).

- Have the students draw a picture of the new word. Encourage the students to write under the picture the sounds they hear in the word.

Change Song

(sing to the tune of "Row, Row, Row Your Boat")

Change, change, change a word,

One sound at a time.

Listening, listening, listening, listening,

Change a sound right now.

(Ask question now)

After final sound change:

"Yes, that's the magic word!"

Magic Word List

man	map	cap	cup
dog	dug	bug	bus
seal	peel	peep	pup
goat	dote	door	deer
bear	bake	sake	sock
moon	mood	rude	red
kite	night	nine	line
nut	nit	fit	fish
hat	hot	fought	fox
mop	cop	cape	cake
lock	log	lug	rug
tire	fire	fine	fan

#50144   *Phonemic Awareness Activities & Games for Early Learners*

Appendix A

Works Cited

Adams, M. Beginning to Read: Thinking and Learning about Print. Cambridge, MA: MIT Press, 1990.

Bradley, L., & Bryant, P. E. "Categorizing sounds and learning to read: A causal connection." Nature, 301 (1983): 419–421.

Center for the Improvement of Early Reading Achievement (CIERA). Put Reading First: The Research Building Blocks for Teaching Children to Read. Urbana-Champaign: University of Illinois, 2001.

Griffith, P. L., & Olson, M. W. "Phonemic awareness helps beginning readers break the code." The Reading Teacher, 45 (1992): 516–523.

Juel, C. "Learning to read and write: A longitudinal study of 54 children from first to fourth grades." Journal of Educational Psychology, 80 (1988): 437–447.

Juel, C., Griffith, P. L., & Gough, P. B. "Acquisition of literacy: A longitudinal study of children in first and second grade." Journal of Educational Psychology, 78 (1986): 243–255.

Lomax, R. G., & McGee, L. M. "Young children's concepts about print and meaning: Toward a model of reading acquisition." Reading Research Quarterly, 22 (1987): 237–256.

Mattingly, I. "Reading, linguistic awareness, and language acquisition." In Language Awareness and Learning to Read, edited by J. Downing & R. Valtin , 9–25. New York: Springer-Verlag, 1984.

Tunmer, W. E., & Nesdale, A. R. "Phonemic segmentation skill and beginning reading." Journal of Educational Psychology, 77 (1985): 417–427.

Yopp, H. K. "Developing phonemic awareness in young children." The Reading Teacher, 45 (1992): 696–703.

Appendix B

Nursery Rhymes

Baa, Baa, Black Sheep

Baa, baa, black sheep
Have you any wool?
No, sir, no, sir,
No bags full;
None to mend the carpets,
None to mend the frocks,
And none to help the little
boy
With holes in his socks.

Fiddle Dee Dee

Fiddle dee dee, fiddle dee
dee,
The fly has married the
bumblebee.
They went to the church,
And married was she.
The fly has married the
bumblebee.

Georgie Porgie

Georgie Porgie, pudding and
pie,
Kissed the girls and made
them cry;
When the boys came out to
play,
Georgie Porgie ran away.

Hickety, Pickety

Hickety, pickety, my black
hen,
She lays eggs for gentlemen;
Gentlemen come every day
To see what my black hen
doth lay.

Hickory, Dickory, Dock

Hickory, dickory, dock,
The mouse ran up the clock.
The clock struck one,
The mouse ran down,
Hickory, dickory, dock.

Hickory, dickory dock,
The mouse ran up the clock.
The clock struck two,
The mouse said "Boo,"
Hickory dickory dock.

Hickory dickory dock,
The mouse ran up the clock.
The clock struck three,
The mouse went "Weeee,"
Hickory dickory dock.

Hickory dickory dock,
The mouse ran up the clock.
The clock struck four,
Let's sing some more,
Hickory dickory dock.

Nursery Rhymes (cont.)

Jack and Jill

Jack and Jill went up the hill,
To fetch a pail of water;
Jack fell down and broke his
crown,
And Jill came tumbling after.
Up Jack got and home did trot,
As fast as he could caper;
Went to bed to mend his head,
With vinegar and brown paper.

Jack Sprat

Jack Sprat could eat no fat,
His wife could eat no lean,
And so betwixt the two of them
They licked the platter clean.

Little Miss Muffet

Little Miss Muffet
Sat on a tuffet,
Eating her curds and whey;
Along came a spider,
And sat down beside her,
And frightened Miss Muffet away.

Little Bo-Peep

Little Bo-Peep has lost her sheep,
And doesn't know where to find
them;
Leave them alone and they'll
come home,
Bringing their tails behind them.
Little Bo-Peep fell fast asleep,
And dreamt she heard them
bleating;
But when she awoke she found it
a joke,
For still they all were fleeting.

Little Jack Horner

Little Jack Horner
Sat in a corner,
Eating his Christmas pie;
He put in his thumb,
And pulled out a plum,
And said "What a good boy am I!"

Mary, Mary, Quite Contrary

Mary, Mary, quite contrary,
How does your garden grow?
With silver bells and cockle shells
And pretty maids all in a row.

Nursery Rhymes (cont.)

Old Mother Hubbard

Old Mother Hubbard
Went to the cupboard,
To get her poor dog a bone;
But when she got there
The cupboard was bare.
And so the poor doggy had none.

Peter, Peter, Pumpkin-Eater

Peter, Peter, pumpkin-eater;
Had a wife and couldn't keep her;
He put her in a pumpkin shell,
And there he kept her very well.

Peter, Peter pumpkin-eater;
Had another and didn't love her;
Peter learned to read and spell,
And then he loved her very well.

Peter Piper

Peter Piper picked a peck of pickled peppers;
A peck of pickled peppers Peter Piper picked.

If Peter Piper picked a peck of pickled peppers,
Where's the peck of pickled peppers Peter Piper picked?

Pease Pudding Hot

Pease pudding hot, pease pudding cold,
Pease pudding in the pot, nine days old.

Some like it hot, some like it cold.
Some like it in the pot nine days old.

Nursery Rhymes (cont.)

Ring-a-ring o'Roses

Ring-a-ring o'roses
A pocket full of posies,
Atishoo! Atishoo!
We all fall down.
Picking up the daises,
Picking up the daises,
Atishoo!, Atishoo!
We all jump up.

Simple Simon

Simple Simon met a pieman
Going to the fair.

Said Simple Simon to the pieman,
"Let me taste your ware."

Said the pieman unto Simon,
"Show me first your penny."

Said Simple Simon to the pieman,
"Indeed I have not any."

Sing a Song of Sixpence

Sing a song of sixpence,
A pocket full of rye;
Four and twenty blackbirds
Baked in a pie.

When the pie was opened,
The birds began to sing;
Now wasn't that a dainty dish
To set before the king?